Small Steps Forward

of related interest

Playing, Laughing and Learning with Children on the Autism Spectrum
A Practical Resource of Play Ideas for Parents and Carers
Julia Moor
ISBN 1 84310 060 6

Giggle Time – Establishing the Social Connection
A Program to Develop the Communication Skills of Children with Autism, Asperger Syndrome and PDD
Susan Aud Sonders
ISBN 1 84310 716 3

Relationship Development Intervention with Young Children
Social and Emotional Development Activities for Asperger Syndrome, Autism, PDD and NLD
Steven E. Gutstein and Rachelle K. Sheely
ISBN 1 84310 714 7

Autism and Play
Jannik Beyer and Lone Gammeltoft
ISBN 1 85302 845 2

Profiles of Play
Assessing and Observing Structure and Process in Play Therapy
Saralea E. Chazan
ISBN 1 84310 703 1

Child Play
Its Importance for Human Development
Peter Slade
ISBN 1 85302 246 2

Small Steps Forward

Using Games and Activities to Help Your
Pre-School Child with Special Needs

Sarah Newman

Illustrated by Jeanie Mellersh

Jessica Kingsley Publishers
London and Philadelphia

First published in the United Kingdom in 1999 by
Jessica Kingsley Publishers
116 Pentonville Road
London N1 9JB, UK
and
400 Market Street, Suite 400
Philadelphia, PA 19106, USA

www.jkp.com

Library of Congress Cataloging-in-Publication Data
Newman, Sarah, 1963–
Games and activities for pre-school children with special needs / Sarah Newman.
p.   cm.
Includes bibliographical references and index.
ISBN 1-85302-643-3 (pb : alk. paper)
1. Handicapped children--Education (Preschool) 2. Developmentally disabled children--Education
(Preschool) 3. Education, Preschool--Activity programs. 4. Educational games. 5. Child
development.
I. Title.
LC4019.2.N48 1999
371.9'0472--dc21
98-45817

British Library Cataloguing in Publication Data
A CIP catalogue record for this book is available from the British Library

ISBN-13: 978 1 85302 643 0
ISBN-10: 1 85302 643 3

Printed and Bound in Great Britain by
Athenaeum Press, Gateshead, Tyne and Wear

Contents

This book is dedicated to my son Christopher

Acknowledgements

I would like to thank the following for their help: Bernie and daughter Claire Barratt; Katherine and children Christopher and Alice Bowell; Lisa and son Jordan Burnell; Tracey and daughter Jade Burrows; Clare and niece Lauren Cooper; Suzannah and Mike and son Daniel Fussell; Sarah and son James Hicks; Liz and son Andrew Hiscox; Richard and Elizabeth and daughter Natasha Jay; Shirley and son Mikey Jones; Peter and son Sebastian Jung; Cheryl and son Alan Maher; Lisa and son Warren Muggleton; Julie and son Liam Ockelford; Julie and son Sam Pursey; Karen and daughter Katy Spurway; Sharon and daughter Georgina Street; Jacolyn and son Declan Thomas; Liz and son Jonathan Washbourn; Lucy and son Jedd Waterton; Jackie and daughter Emily Whitley; Deidre and son Oliver Witherby; Julie and Tom and daughter Alice Wood.

I would also like to thank the following for giving their professional advice: Ann Baker, Joan Turnbull Opportunity Group; Jasia Beaumont, Sleep Clinic Nurse; Jane Davey, Citizens Advice Bureau; Jane Dutton, Hardmoor Early Years Centre; Lucinda Edwards, Avon Valley Opportunity Group; Caroline Evans, Portage Home Visitor; Sue Evans, Social Worker; Emma Gibbs, Educational Psychologist; Dr Neil Harris, Consultant Child Psychiatrist; Dr Jo Lee, GP; Ally Levell, Joan Turnbull Opportunity Group; Ingrid Marcham, Joan Turnbull Opportunity Group; Liz Matthew, Occupational Therapist; Irene Osman, Swimming Instructor; Jenny Powell, Occupational Therapist; David Reid, Parent Partnership Service, Hampshire County Council; Lyn Rollison, Portage Home Visitor; Dr Carolyn Smith, Educational Psychologist; Dr Kara Tanaga, GP; Katrina Watt, Fortune Centre of Riding Therapy and Cynthia Wilson, Music Teacher.

I would like to thank the Makaton Vocabulary Development Project for allowing me to reproduce the sign and symbols for cat and biscuit on page 106.

I would like to thank all the children, some with special needs and some without who modelled for the illustrations in the book.

My very special thanks are due to the following who gave me a lot of time and help: Pam Gammer, Senior Portage Home Visitor; Sally Goodson, Speech and Language Therapist; Katya Gorman, Occupational Therapist; Jenny Gurd, Supervisor, Joan Turnbull Opportunity Group; Kenzie Revington, Physiotherapist and Dr Valerie Shrubb FRCPCH, Consultant Paediatrician.

I would like to thank Sharon Brien, Jackie Donnellan, Jenny Ladbury, Jo Strudwick, my brother James and my parents who all helped in different ways. I would also like to thank Jeanie Mellersh for her wonderful illustrations. She was a constant source of ideas, encouragement and support. Thanks also to Nick Mellersh for all his help. Above all I would like to thank David for all his help and encouragement.

Foreword

Just before Christopher's first birthday, we took him to see a paediatrician because he was failing to reach his developmental milestones. We were told that he was developmentally delayed and that he would need all sorts of tests, including genetic tests and a brain scan to see if a diagnosis could be reached. We were fortunate in that Christopher started at an Opportunity Group within a week, and that eventually he received all sorts of help including portage, riding, speech and occupational therapy. I find it impossible to think back to that time without remembering the utter desperation, despair and inadequacy my partner David and I felt at the news and in the months to come. Christopher was our first child and the pregnancy and birth had seemed to go well. Christopher was slow to develop but we thought it was just that – slowness – and had not imagined that he had serious developmental problems. Looking back now, having had two more sons – Nicholas and William – I can see that Christopher was different from birth, but that is another story. At one Christopher couldn't sit up, he didn't make eye contact and rarely showed any interest in anything or anybody apart from a set of keys.

Having discovered there was a problem, I wanted to find out what I could do to help him develop and move on. I looked for books but could not find anything that looked at very early skills in an approachable way. Christopher had no diagnosis so it was impossible to tap into the different organizations around. In the end, I just badgered different professionals to give me suggestions – work on eye contact, work on object permanence etc. It helped me to feel I was doing something and it certainly helped him. From about 20 months he started to make real progress and has continued to do so to date. Now, at four and a half, he is even beginning to talk! In the same way when I have had to tackle major issues like toileting or claims for Disability Living Allowance I have asked Pam (my portage home visitor) or

Jenny (Opportunity Group Supervisor) for information and advice. Despite busy schedules they have always found time to talk to me. I don't know what I would have done without them.

One day, just before Christopher was three, Pam unloaded her bag of toys in the sitting room and out tumbled some books on games for children. She said that one of her 'mums' wanted some ideas for games, so she had found some books for ordinary children which she could use by adapting the games to a more appropriate level. It was from that moment that the idea came to me of writing a book for parents of children with special needs, the kind of book that I had sought and been unable to find. It would show how development proceeded so that parents would know where their child is and where he or she is heading. I also wanted to produce a book which wasn't specific to a certain condition because many young children don't have a diagnosis and also because, even if they do, their problems often span a number of developmental areas. It would give ideas for easy games and activities and it would also give the theory behind those common problems of childhood like sleeping and behaviour management.

Shortly after my starting to write this book, Christopher received the diagnosis of autism. The irony is that I had said originally that I could cope with anything except autism. But here I am. I have coped!

HOW THE BOOK IS STRUCTURED

Ordinary children are programmed to learn and develop. They are always investigating and exploring while they play and are always processing the information they discover to make sense of the world. They are responsive, interested and motivated and endlessly creative, constantly testing and assimilating what they have learnt. They have the means and the motivation to be constantly moving forward and they can demand from adults the support and information they need.

For children with special needs it is often not so easy. In one way or another you have to give them more help and encouragement, whether it is stimulation, motivation, inform-ation or support. In some development areas you have to introduce the next step, extending your children's play and helping them with specific problems. Therefore you have to have an understanding of their developmental stage and what you expect them to do next so that you can help them move forward in small steps to reach their full potential.

The book has therefore been written to give you an idea of the progression of child development so that you can see where your child is and where he or she is heading. It starts off with how to cope with having a child with special needs and then moves on to give general advice on how to play with your child. The core of the book divides child development into the following areas: cognitive, language, physical, sensory, social and emotional, because these are the most easily understood. However, these divisions are somewhat artificial. All areas of development are inter-related and therefore there is a lot of repetition of skills like turn-taking, object permanence and copying, which are relevant to more than one area.

Each chapter takes one developmental area and describes a child's progression and then suggests a variety of games and activities to help stimulate the child along the way. The child's progression is further subdivided into chronological develop-ment which describes the order in which skills are gained and parallel development for those skills which develop continuously alongside each other.

Following this, Chapter 9, Additional Practical Advice, gives information on tackling the issues of behaviour management, sleep and toileting. Chapter 10, The Support Your Child Should Expect, gives information on the support that is available, including the roles of professionals, the statutory assessment process and sources of financial help. Chapter 11, Resources, gives ideas if you require further information including a bibliography and addresses of voluntary organizations.

HOW TO USE THIS BOOK

I have not written this book to tell you what you *should* be doing with your child. It is only to give you some ideas of games if you *want* to do something more structured. In no way do I want to make you feel any more pressure. There will be many times when you just want to have fun with your child in a completely free way. On those occasions you should leave this book on the shelf.

Don't try to read this book in one go. Read Chapter 1, How To Survive, if you need to. Then read Chapter 2, What Everyone Needs To Know, and the sections which are relevant to your child. If you were to try to read it all at once you would probably just feel overwhelmed. It is not designed to cover one moment in time but to cover years of development. Concentrate on the sections which are relevant to your child at a particular time and then look again in a few months' time as your child develops.

Remember that not all the ideas will work for all children. Use and adapt what you think will work for your child.

I have deliberately not put any reference to the age at which children are expected to achieve skills. Such age guidelines are vague – just compare the different skills of a group of one-year-olds. I believe that it is important for parents to be aware of the progress their child is making, however small, but it does not help to make comparisons with their child's peers. If you do want to know, there are many excellent books which give indications of ages. See the bibliography in Chapter 11, Resources.

This book is inevitably a starting point if you find your child has special needs and you want to do something constructive in the first few months and years. If in time you need more specialist information and advice, refer to the organizations and books listed in Chapter 11, Resources.

Please note

1. I have included quotes from parents about their experiences.

2. Sometimes the child's name has been changed.

3. I have used the terms 'he' and 'she' interchangeably to represent your child.

4. I have written this book from the standpoint of a family consisting of a mother and father. However, I appreciate that this is not always the case, and hope that the many lone parents who may be reading this book will have no difficulty in adapting the ideas and activities to their circumstances.

5. When making toys or using household objects as toys, make sure they are safe and appropriate for your child.

6. If you are concerned about any area of your child's development seek advice from your health visitor or general practitioner. They should be able to help you or refer you to someone more appropriate.

CHAPTER 1

How to Survive

This section reflects how I have felt and how I have coped with my own situation but also draws on many of the experiences other parents have told me about. You may not recognize the emotions I talk about and may have found other ways of surviving. You may find it too recent and too raw. I wish I had known this when my child was diagnosed as having special needs but I suspect you have to live through it all to be able to feel this way.

First of all, parents have to admit that their child does have a problem. It can take many parents a long time before they can accept this.

For most parents it is a terrible shock when they realize they have a child with special needs and they experience a period of sadness and even desolation and desperation as they try to work through what it means now and for the future.

I felt totally and utterly destroyed by the news of Christopher's problems. I felt inadequate and unprepared. I felt guilty in case I was in some way responsible, I felt it was punishment for making glib assumptions about Christopher – 'when he goes to university', 'when he leaves home', etc. I had no idea what the future held for him – whether he would even walk or talk. I didn't know what the consequences would be for my partner and I – whether we could risk having any more children, whether we would always have a dependent and embarrassing son with us. All those happy, cosy, 'normal' assumptions had gone out of the window and I was left with an incredible sadness, a feeling of being totally alone, even though I have a wonderfully supportive partner and family, and a sense of inadequacy about facing the future and all its terrible uncertainties. And yet I still had this little chap whom I loved and who was totally dependent on me and through it all I had to continue caring for him and I suppose that is the way I got through it – by looking after and loving my own child as he was and learning to take each day at a time.

Despite what people say, you never 'get over' finding out that your child has special needs. The hurt will always be with you and the problems and difficulties, though they may change, will always be present. However, most parents find a way of dealing with it on a daily basis and thereby come to some sort of acceptance of what it means for them and their child.

COMING TO TERMS WITH YOUR CHILD'S SITUATION

Finding out that your child has special needs is a devastating experience which stays with you for the rest of your life. It never ceases to be with you and to affect everything you do and think about your child and everything else as well. Many people find themselves profoundly changed by the experience. On the negative side, they are more bitter and angry but, on the positive side, they are more tolerant of weakness and more in tune with what's important in life.

I felt I went through a kind of grieving process when I found my son had special needs – a mourning for a child I thought I had, for lost expectations, hopes and assumptions. Christopher was one year old when we found out he had significant problems and we didn't know if he would walk or talk, let alone go to the local school or leave home. It takes a long time to come to terms with your child's situation, to feel at ease with all the unknowns and able to move on to look to the future. I felt it took about six months before I was on a fairly even keel but even now, several years on, I still can get upset by memories, by seeing normal children doing normal things or by careless comments by other parents. The struggle of everyday life can also be overwhelming at times. I felt I changed. I now make fewer assumptions about life and, I hope, am less judgemental and more accepting of people and situations.

Strategies

Hold on to how much you **love your child,** how much he needs you and you him. Enjoy him. Think of him first as the child you want and love and second as someone with special needs.

When I came back from hospital with Matthew after his diagnosis I remember thinking that there was no point talking to him because I thought that he was a 'vegetable'. The feeling lasted for a few hours only and then I was back in the instinctive role of loving and caring for my child. It is quite frightening to look back and see how negative I felt.

Take one day at a time and don't try to look too far into the future. Deal with your child as he is now and will be in the next few days and weeks. Who knows what any child will be like five or ten years hence?

Move forward. Concentrate on the improvements and the progress your child is making however slow, rather than on any comparison with his peers.

HOW TO STAY SANE

Having children is hard work and having children with special needs can be harder still. Parents have to provide a lot of care, maybe carrying out medical procedures, and they have to do a lot more hands-on playing. All this has to be incorporated into a busy day. Children with special needs often have behavioural problems which are stressful for their parents. Just carrying and moving children who are unable to walk is physically demanding and there is often extra washing and cleaning. Daily life is quickly taken up with appointments at hospitals, with therapists and getting to and from playgroups. Finally, there can be considerable stress both in negotiating with the professional services to get the best for a child now, and in contemplating what the future holds.

I don't think it is generally recognized how hard things can be for parents of children with special needs. If you ask friends and family with children how they view their lives they will tell you that their lives are tough. I know that when I found things very hard this response made me feel totally inadequate. Their lives were tough but they were coping, I wasn't. It was only later when I had another child that I realized that I wasn't inadequate and that life with a child with special needs is very different and very difficult.

Parents often don't get much positive encouragement. Friends and family rarely tell parents that they are doing a good job raising their children. If they are seen to cope then people assume

Having children is hard work

they are okay and do not need support and encouragement. So the onus is largely on parents themselves to recognize when they need help and support and to demand it. Parents feel that they should be able to cope on their own, so when they do give in and ask for support they feel as if they have failed. Added to this, other parents often look askance when they hear of the support available, such as playgroups and respite care, and even tell parents of children with special needs how 'lucky they are'.

Strategies

° Resist attempts to be heroic. Be realistic. Remember that only you know your child, your circumstances and your needs. **Take any help you can get** from family, friends, social services etc. whether it is help in the house or respite care for your child. If you send your child to a childminder, make sure your child is secure and comfortable, that the childminder has confidence that she can understand and deal with your child's needs and that you feel totally happy with the arrangement. Start by leaving your child for an hour or so and build up to whatever you need. Find an arrangement that suits you. Your child could go to the carer's house or the carer could come to you if it makes you more comfortable. Your child will also benefit from the different experience, environment and people – so everyone wins.

○ Seriously **consider any opportunities that are offered to your child**, such as a place at an Opportunity Group or Child Development Centre. These places can be frightening for parents because they force them to confront the fact that their child has special needs and that he may be placed with other children who have different and maybe more severe needs. However, if your child may benefit from the experience it is worth trying.

○ **Find local networks of parents in similar situations.** There are many ways for parents to meet other parents who have faced similar experiences, for example through parent support groups, Child Development Centres or national organizations with local branches (see Chapter 11). Alternatively you can ask your doctors or therapists to help you make contact with parents of children with similar special needs. You probably won't like everyone you meet but if you make an effort you may make some good friends. It can be helpful and reassuring to meet parents who have been there before and survived. If you meet parents of children with the same or similar problems to yours you can also share useful information, concerns and ideas. If they are a bit further down the line with an older child they can give you an idea of future issues like schooling. (However, some parents find it disturbing to meet children much older than their own or with more severe problems.) It can also be much more relaxing visiting people whose children have special needs since they are more understanding of odd behaviour and their houses are often geared up more appropriately. Neither side feels they have to make constant excuses and apologies for their children.

○ **Take time out for yourself.** What you want to do may not seem very important compared to your child's needs but if it makes you feel better about yourself, more rested and invigorated, it is well worth doing. For some it might be a swim or a walk, for others the chance to read a book in peace or to go shopping and be able to try on clothes. Find time to do whatever you want by sending your child to respite care or friends. If you have a break, you will return to your child feeling refreshed, you will feel better about yourself and be able to give more to your child.

Find time to do what you want

- ° If you feel overloaded by appointments and commitments, remember **it is okay to say 'no' to professionals.** Sometimes if your child has special needs and associated medical problems you can feel that you are looking after a medical 'case' rather than caring for your own child. Professionals need to know what your daily life and responsibilities are and adjust their expectations accordingly. If you feel overwhelmed, ask which is the most important issue and deal with that alone. Alternatively, take a break, have time just to enjoy your child and then come back to all the playgroups and therapies when you are ready.

- ° **Don't feel guilty about saying 'no' to your child** if you can't do something or don't want to do something he wants to do. You have as much right as he has to choose activities and you also have a view of your day and domestic responsibilities which your child cannot have. If your child wants to paint and it is going to make a terrible mess which you don't want to or haven't time to clear up, say 'no'. Children have to learn that their desires cannot be met in full all the time because they have to consider the needs and wishes of others. It only becomes a problem if you do it too often. You also have to remember that they then have a right to say 'no' to you!

HOW MUCH PARENTS CAN DO

Parents are in a unique position with regard to their child. They are usually with him the most and know him best. They are the most important people in his life. By stimulating him, by providing security and support, by seeking help for him, by following his progress and moving him on and above all by loving him, they help their child develop.

Parents should have confidence in their skills and abilities as parents and have the courage to rely on their intuitive understanding of their child's needs and desires. Finding out that a child has special needs can knock a parent's confidence, particularly if the diagnosis comes as a total surprise. When a child is the subject of a stream of therapists and consultants the idea that parenting is a natural and innate skill can seem implausible. If it takes a team of professional experts to help a child learn to sit up and eat his food, what role does an amateur parent have? Parents play a vital role and the best care a child can receive is when parents and professionals work together with a true understanding of a child's needs. Therapists may suggest an approach but a parent will probably have an instinctive view of whether it is likely to work or not or how it should be modified to suit their particular child. Parents who trust their instincts and play with their child in a way that feels right for them and their child are usually right. Because parents know their child so well, they will also know when things aren't right and seek help.

A child does not exist in isolation – he is always part of a relationship, with his mother, his father and his siblings. Relationships are about two people not just one. So when looking at a child's needs, those of the parents need to be considered too. A child who is cared for tirelessly by a mother who ignores her own needs is not in a healthy relationship. On the other hand a mother who is gaining something from her child and from time away from her child is happier and more confident, and of course ultimately gives more to the child. When you think about your child's needs you must remember your own needs too.

Parents who are motivated, interested and tenacious can sometimes do amazing things for their child with special needs. However, before selflessly dedicating their lives to their child they should look carefully at the wider issues and their other responsibilities:

Personal needs

Many new parents feel that a continuous round of feeding, changing, bathing and cuddling has swallowed up all their time and opportunities to pursue former interests. Gradually the chance to do aerobics or read books returns as life becomes a bit easier. But having a child with special needs can make parents feel particularly guilty about taking time away from their child to do something which they find satisfying but which seems in the context to be rather frivolous. Such parents inevitably have less time for themselves but it is important that they do make time to do something for their own personal enjoyment and self-esteem.

Relationship with partner and other family members

Parents need to make time to ensure that their relationships with their partner, their own parents and other family members can still flourish.

Other children

When parents have other children, it can be very difficult to get the balance of attention right. Inevitably a child with special needs will require more attention, special equipment and hospital visits but a way has to be found of showing the other children that they are loved and valued and that their own needs are recognized. A lot depends on the individual situation and the special needs involved but respite care or family help can be used to give time alone with other children. It may be worth making sure that each child has at least one special activity of his or her own choice. It is very dangerous to get so wrapped up in the problems of one child that problems with others go unrecognized. The resentment that some siblings feel for the way their parents devoted all their time and energy to their disabled brother or sister and not to them can last for years, sometimes for ever.

Financial needs

Their financial situation may mean parents have to work full- or part-time and thus limit the amount of time they can spend with their children.

Parents' role

Parents have a role in helping their child's development but they are not working to a syllabus which has to be completed within a set time limit. Their role is wider than that of a teacher. They provide a base of unconditional love. Whatever children achieve or do not achieve parents will still love and care for them. Parents can simply enjoy being with their child, doing something or nothing, introducing him to new experiences or revisiting old and favourite ones. They provide a secure environment where a child can be confident and happy, not one where he is constantly being tested and stretched.

The phrase **'Good enough mother/father'** is worth remembering.[1] Parents want to do everything possible to help their child and it is very easy for them to feel that they are not doing 'enough' and that they are not perfect. But such feelings do not help anyone – the child or the parent. A 'good enough mother/father' is what parents are and all they have to be.

> All the specialists bombard you with leaflets and things to do and you feel as if you should be doing everything all at once and that you are never doing enough. Also there seems little reward especially when your child is unresponsive. I read somewhere: **Whatever you do is enough.**

RELATIONSHIP WITH YOUR PARTNER

Having a baby puts many relationships under strain as each person adjusts to his or her new role and the changed relationship. In particular, fathers can feel excluded by the close emotional and physical bond between mother and baby. In addition, the mother may feel that she has the whole burden of looking after the child while the father feels that he is doing his bit bringing in his salary. If he is unable to attend appointments and to see his child with his peers he may also have more difficulty accepting his child has special needs at all. Finding out you have a child with special needs means unhappiness and additional stress for you and for your partner. The experience will throw a sharp spotlight on all aspects of a relationship and open

1   See Winnicott, D.W. (1971) *Playing and Reality.* London: Routledge.

up areas of weakness or disagreement which in normal circumstances might have gone undetected.

Strategies

° **Listen to each other** and respect each other's feelings and views. The mother, if she is the main carer, can sometimes feel that she knows her child best but the father has a unique position and a valid viewpoint and should not be ignored.

° **Don't make assumptions** about your partner. Find out what your partner thinks about important issues, don't just assume that you know how he or she feels.

° Remember that **different people come to terms with situations in different ways.** Your partner may not be showing his grief in the same way as you but it does not mean that he feels it any less than you.

° **Don't fall into the trap of making your views more extreme than they really are** in order to contradict your partner's view. Sometimes one partner can paint a very dire picture of the situation, making the other take a more upbeat view than he or she really feels and irritating the first into even more extreme views. You can find your views and selves polarized and it can feel as if one partner is refusing to accept there is a problem. If you were being honest you would probably accept that neither is saying what he or she really thinks and that your views are closer than they appear. This problem can be exacerbated by the fact that parents often have very little information to go on about their child's condition. Seek out more information so that you can both come to a better understanding.

° **Help each other out.** Try to ensure that family responsibilities have been divided reasonably and that both partners are doing their fair share. Each couple will work things out differently according to preferences and situation. If you really cannot help in one area make sure you take the burden in other areas.

> I look after the children full-time and John goes to work full-time. I don't mind at all because I know when he comes home at 6pm he takes over completely and gives them baths and puts them to bed. Meanwhile I clear up and cook our supper. Once supper is over John washes up and clears away

and my evening starts. We have an ironing lady so that I don't feel I have piles of ironing hanging over me every evening and we do the absolute minimum of cleaning. It seems to work.

○ **Be prepared to rethink your lifestyle radically.** People often have preconceptions about how they are going to cope when they have children, whether the mother will go back to work, whether they can still go trekking round the Himalayas and how they will divide up household chores. Things rarely turn out as they think they will. When a child has special needs, things are usually more difficult and you have to be prepared to look at your situation objectively, decide on priorities and take appropriate action. Working long hours away from home with a long commute might put too much of a strain on the main carer and the working partner may have to seek work which allows him or her to spend more time at home.

○ **Find time to be together without the children.** Get a baby-sitter and go out somewhere, even if it is just to the local pub for a chat for an hour or so. Talk about your views on your child's situation and what it means for your partner and for you. Also make sure you talk about things other than your child to give you a chance to rebalance your relationship.

RELATIONSHIP WITH FAMILY AND FRIENDS

Parents usually look to their own family and friends to give them support when they find out that they have a child with special needs. Inevitably some people will be more sensitive and aware and give better support than others.

Family

Coming from a different generation, grandparents have grown up when attitudes to children with special needs were quite different. The fact that thirty years ago children with special needs were largely considered ineducable shows how far we have come. Unless they already have direct experience of children with special needs, grandparents may well need to change their own attitudes. They will also have to face the reactions of their contemporaries. In addition, they have to come to terms with their own sadness about the news of their grandchild and their disappointed dreams. Parents can often feel that rather than getting any support from their own parents they are having to prop them up as well.

Some parents find that their families can focus exclusively on the 'problem' and forget that there is a child in there too. This is particularly true when special needs are identified at birth. Parents still want time to celebrate and enjoy the birth of a new and wonderful baby and do not want to be forever reminded of the problems ahead.

On the other hand, some grandparents may refuse to accept that there is a problem, never allude to it and dismiss your efforts to get help. Tell them that they are not being helpful to you or your child.

> I have always found the best policy is to be entirely open about Vicky's problems because I feel if you don't recognize the problem you don't appreciate the achievements.

Relationships with grandparents vary enormously but if you have good relationships then it is worth keeping the grandparents informed and getting them involved. Grandparents are in a unique position of trust, love and involvement and so can be a great source of help. Having a different lifestyle they can also access different information and advice. On the other hand, as they probably have a lot more time than you, they can sometimes add to your stress with such questions as 'Have you contacted so-and- so yet?' or 'Have you read that article yet?'

Friends

People generally are not very good at talking to those in highly charged emotional situations. They often find it so difficult to say something appropriate that they end up saying nothing – which can be more hurtful because most people facing grief or loss prefer to talk about it.

> I have very strong memories of a dinner party with friends from my ante-natal group held two weeks after Elizabeth's first diagnosis. We talked about all the children but Elizabeth was carefully ignored. I remember feeling as if I did not really exist. My whole being was consumed by this concern and love for my daughter and this devastating news and yet I wasn't allowed to talk about it. Later I realized that it was up to me to talk about it.

Now, if I set the tone by talking about my child, saying what was happening and what she was doing, my friends respond really well.

If you don't talk about your child your friends will assume you don't want to and keep quiet themselves. Good friends are an enormous source of strength and support so try to get the relationship to work.

HOW TO COPE WITH PUBLIC REACTIONS

While researching this book it became clear that many parents had experienced some awful reactions from people because of the appearance or behaviour of their child.

Everyone responds to such reactions differently according to circumstances, the child involved, their own personality and how they feel on any given day. There is no right response. Sometimes you feel brave and strong and are able to challenge people's assumptions and rudeness; other times you just move on and away as quickly as you can, often wishing afterwards that you could have thought of a witty put-down.

Alternatively you can meet people who think they are being helpful by being terribly positive or over-sympathetic. They make comments like 'Oh well, he looks all right to me', 'Oh, but my child does that as well' or 'Oh, how terrible for you'.

Strategies

° Remember **your primary duty is to your child** and not to educate other people in equal opportunities and common humanity. Keep your child safe and keep doing what you need to do in order to help your child in the long term. If other people cannot handle this then it is their problem and not yours.

° If someone makes an adverse comment, you could try saying something like 'I'm sorry you find Amy's behaviour distressing but she does have cerebral palsy/autism/a heart condition' and then move away quickly.

If Laura starts misbehaving and I detect hostility, I start using sign language to her in a very exaggerated way, so that people can pick up on the fact that she has special needs. They then either back off immediately or very occasionally ask if she is deaf or talk about signing.

° It is important to lead as 'normal' a life as possible for your own sake and for that of all your children. You must go out, go shopping, go to the park and visit people. However it is sensible to know your own limits and those of your child. **There is no point making yourself miserable to prove a point.** Some shops are geared up for children and have helpful and understanding staff, try to avoid ones which aren't. Some days you may feel up to going out and about with your child, other days you may be feeling fragile and prefer to stay at home. Be realistic. When you have children, certain activities become difficult or impossible. Just make sure you do have time through respite care or family help to do things that are important to you.

° **Be careful not to jump to conclusions about people's attitudes** towards you and your child. It is very easy when you are out with your child who is drawing attention to himself to think that people are condemning you as an ineffective parent and your child as badly behaved. Sometimes you know because they say as much but other times they may merely be looking at you out of curiosity and feeling sympathy and support.

> I live in a small village where I frequently go shopping with my two children. In the grocer's Tom has an obsession with the dog food, the Frosties and cucumbers, in the Post Office with the batteries and in the newsagent with the chilled drinks cabinet. One day I had a miserable time doing battle in each of these shops trying to stop Tom pulling things off the shelf and wrecking everything. I felt the shopkeepers and customers were staring at me disapprovingly and at Tom in horror. I seriously wondered if it was feasible to go shopping again with him. The next day I went in on my own and Karen in the newsagent amazed me by asking me where I found the energy to deal with Tom and commenting on how much he had improved. She noticed that he used signs (Makaton) and asked to be taught how to say 'hello' to him. Rather than being disapproving she had actually been really supportive and I had completely misjudged her and probably many others.

When I see other parents having 'problems' with their child's behaviour, I try to 'look supportive' but they probably interpret my look as one of a smug and judgemental mother. It is very difficult to show solidarity and support without appearing nosy and interfering.

DIAGNOSIS

When parents first find out that their child has special needs they rarely get an immediate and specific diagnosis of, say, dyspraxia or cerebral palsy, but are more likely to receive a label of global developmental delay, communication delay or something else equally vague and non-specific. It may take months if not years to get a full diagnosis and many never receive one at all.

A diagnosis can seem vitally important. Parents hope that it will provide the 'answer' to their child's problems – a blueprint for how to treat the child and a vision of what the future holds. Equally, parents are often concerned that they are responsible in some way for their child's condition and therefore want to know the 'cause' to eradicate the suspicion of guilt. They may also need to know if there are any genetic implications which may affect their decision whether or not to have more children. On the other hand, while there is no diagnosis the hope may remain that the doctors have got it wrong.

A diagnosis is useful in many ways. After the initial shock, parents can start to come to terms with their child's condition and his situation. It can be a low point, but once they know the worst, they can move on, start looking forward and be positive. It can make things easier with other people. If you say your child has 'special needs' with no diagnosis you may be regarded as a neurotic parent by some people or as a parent who is making excuses for his or her child's poor performance or behaviour.

> In our case saying our son is autistic seems a lot more acceptable as an excuse for extraordinary behaviour than saying he has special needs.

As parents you can start to access organizations and help groups relevant to your child's special needs. These can provide extremely useful support, information and ideas and access to other parents in similar situations.

There is a perception that having a diagnosis helps with the provision of services by health and education, but this should not be the case since children should be considered on the basis of their needs not by their label.

However, if you do have a diagnosis, remember the points below. Equally, if you don't have a diagnosis, consider these before expending huge amounts of money and energy on seeking one.

A child with special needs is a unique individual and should always be considered in this way. You should always think about the child and not the label. The kind of support and education he requires will be determined by his needs alone. A diagnosis can push children down a particular route for care or education which may not be appropriate. Just because children with Down's Syndrome generally follow a certain developmental pattern it does not follow that every child with Down's Syndrome will. The usual approach may not be appropriate for your child.

Similarly most 'labels' cover such a huge spectrum of abilities that they don't actually give you any real clue as to what the future holds, let alone a blueprint. Only think of the range of abilities within the spectrum of autism, Down's Syndrome or cerebral palsy. A diagnosis may give you access to more information, but parents still have to search for help, labour over decisions and wait and see how things unfold.

> I found out Christopher had special needs when he was one, and then when he was three, at a routine meeting with his consultant, we were given a working diagnosis of autism. I remember thinking with relief 'Oh so that's what you call Christopher'. Get the label to fit the child – do not force the child to fit the label.

Some parents get hung up on searching for a diagnosis. A child won't be any different just because he has a convenient label. In the end it is just a label and energies are probably better spent on other activities.

CHAPTER 2

What Everyone Needs to Know

INTRODUCTION

This chapter looks at those general issues which are important for all children whatever their special needs and whatever they are doing. It looks at the environment and how to make it conducive to play; it also details how to arrange activities so that your child has a greater chance of success. It looks at how to motivate your child and other general issues which are important for children with special needs.

CREATING THE RIGHT ENVIRONMENT FOR PLAY

All children are easily distracted by activities and objects around them. In addition, if they have little interest in what they are doing or have physical problems which make concentrating difficult, they may be particularly flitty. It is therefore important to create an environment which is as conducive as possible to learning. Consider the following aspects of the environment:

Timing

Find a time to play with your child when she is alert and happy, not hungry or tired and when you have time, energy and enthusiasm to devote to her. Choose a time when you are unlikely to be disturbed and when you are not distracted by other tasks. You are then more likely to get a positive response.

Noise

Having a television, radio or music on, while doing other things, makes it more difficult to concentrate. If you are trying to play constructively with your child it is a good idea to turn everything off and let her concentrate. If she has a hearing loss or a language problem this is doubly important because she will need to concentrate on what you are saying and will find it very difficult if noise from elsewhere is competing.

Distractions

When you play with your child, clear the table or floor space of clutter and unnecessary toys. Keep out only the toy you are playing with. As you finish with toys do not leave them lying around but put them away, out of sight in a box or bag. This way your child will not be distracted by the next or previous activity and will be more likely to stay on track.

Some children can be easily distracted

Clear the table of any unnecessary toys

If you have a child who is very easily distracted and who fiddles with everything, keep your house as free of clutter as you can. Some children can be very easily distracted by things such as toys, ornaments and household goods and you may have to make quite drastic changes to aid concentration.

Working at the dining table or on a low table may help because it will be more difficult for your child to see other distractions and to run away.

To minimize distractions, you could consider creating a 'work bay' for your child in your house like ones often used in special schools. In these schools children often work at a table which is placed in a bay with high plain walls on three sides so they cannot see out and are therefore encouraged to concentrate on the activities given to them. Children learn the idea of working from left to right because tasks are placed on their left; they then work on them and move them to the right once completed. This may seem a very drastic measure for the home but you can use the idea of placing a table in a quiet corner against plain walls. Some children respond well to having a specific place for 'working'. The idea of a 'work bay' is particularly used in TEACCH, which is a programme devised in the USA for children with autism and communication disorders.[1]

Seating

Many children will play and concentrate very happily while sitting on the floor or at a conventional table. However, if your child has a physical disability of any kind then her position and seating should be considered.

A child who is poorly positioned so that she feels un-comfortable, insecure or unsupported will be concentrating on stabilizing herself rather than doing any other activity you give her. If she is using her hands to prop herself up, she will not be able to use them to play. A child, on the other hand, who is comfortable and properly supported will be in a good position to play and free to concentrate on learning new skills. Equally, a child who is extremely fidgety will benefit from proper seating because she will be encouraged to sit still and because she will find it more difficult to escape and evade you.

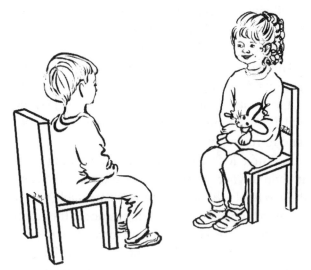

Correct sitting position

1   TEACCH (Treatment and Education of Autistic and related Communication-handicapped CHildren) can be contacted at Division TEACCH Administration and Research, CB 7180, 310 Medical School Wing E, The University of North Carolina at Chapel Hill, Chapel Hill, North Carolina 27599-7180, USA; Tel 001 919 966 2173.

There are all sorts of seating options you could think about including a specialist chair, a low table and chair, a high chair or a chair at the dining table. Consider your child's particular circumstances and discuss any requirements with your occupational therapist.

On the other hand, if balance is not a problem, it is often good to experiment with different seating positions because they can help with physical skills. Playing on the floor, at a table or when kneeling at a coffee table, requires different postures and develops different muscles.

Lighting

Good bright lighting is important for everyone and for a child with a visual impairment clear bright light is vital to allow her to use and develop the sight that she has. Also when you are talking or playing with your child, avoid standing in front of a window with your face in darkness.

Your position when playing with your child

Always sit directly opposite your child when playing with her and talking to her. It will then be easy for her to make eye contact with you, to see your face, mouth, eyes and expression and to see what you are doing and to copy it. If you sit next to her, you will make it more difficult for her to see what you are doing since she will only get a sideways view and will not be able to see your face very easily. The same advice holds for other non-play situations, for instance if you are trying to teach your child to feed herself, turn her high chair to face you directly rather than have her sit alongside you.

MAKE ACTIVITIES ACHIEVABLE

Devise activities which your child has a chance of completing. The following sections show ways of doing this.

Break skills down into small steps

You can make things easier for your child by breaking new skills down into smaller and more manageable steps. Rather than

trying to teach a new skill in one go, aim to get there gradually.
For example, if you want to get your child to feed herself with a
spoon, start by loading a spoon with food, then get her to lift the
spoon to her mouth, probably by placing your hand over hers
and taking it to her mouth. Then when she can do that, get her to
put the spoon back in the bowl and finally to scoop the food onto
the spoon.

Similarly, if you are potty training your child start by
concentrating on getting her to wee or poo in the potty and do
the other bits like undressing, bottom wiping, dressing and
handwashing for her. As she becomes ready you can get her to
take on more of the process. She might then become able to pull
her trousers or tights down, later pull them up again and wash her
hands until finally she is able to do the whole routine with
guidance and ultimately independently.

Start by making things easy

Introduce any new skill by using toys which are easy for your
child to use and understand. Then as she becomes more
competent, gradually make the games more challenging for her.
So don't get out your 2000-piece jigsaw puzzle when you want
to play with puzzles but find one with two or three pieces. Find
chunky blocks to thread with a thick and firm cord before
moving on to cotton reels and beads using a flimsy cord. If you
are concentrating on feeding with a spoon, start with food like
yoghurt which sticks to the spoon and then progress slowly to
more difficult consistencies like pasta or thin soups.

Start with objects which fit comfortably into your child's hand
and which she can manipulate easily. Very large objects can be as
difficult to handle as very tiny ones.

Forward and backward chaining

There are also two useful techniques called forward and
backward chaining. Think of an activity as a chain or sequence of
tiny actions. Forward chaining is when you get a child to perform
the first action in the sequence which you then complete, and
backward chaining is when you get a child to perform the last
action in the sequence which you have started. You then

gradually increase the amount your child has to do as she becomes more competent until she is doing the whole thing.

For instance, if you want your child to wash her face you might use forward chaining. Get her to start by putting her hands in the water, then you finish the action yourself. As she becomes more able get her to bring her hands to her face, then wash it and later still dry it. Alternatively, if you want your child to build a tower, use forward chaining by getting her to place the first brick on the floor and then place the bricks on top yourself. Then get her to place another brick on the bottom one and then complete the tower yourself. Gradually, get her to build more of the tower with you doing the top fiddly bricks until she is able to do them all.

If you want your child to do a jigsaw puzzle use backward chaining. Complete the puzzle except for the very last piece. Then get your child to put in the last piece so she gets all the reward and praise for completing the puzzle. Then as she improves, get her to insert more pieces. The point is that you want her to feel the greatest sense of achievement at the earliest

Backward chaining: put the last piece in the jigsaw

possible opportunity. Choose the chaining method which enables her to do the easy bit and then build on her success.

Be aware of where your child is developmentally

Follow your child's developmental progress and see what sort of skills she should be working towards. If you give your child something to do which is way beyond her she will have little chance of success, quickly lose interest and become frustrated and angry.

MOTIVATION
Use your child's interests

Children with special needs often do not have a great urge to explore and experiment with toys. They may need to be given the motivation to learn. You can use your understanding of what interests and excites your child to provide the motivation.

Most skills can be learned in a variety of situations and the key to success is often picking the right way of introducing a new idea or skill. Putting objects in a box is a very important skill but it is deeply unexciting. You can make it more interesting by using objects which make a good noise as they hit the container or by holding the box and making the objects jump out after they have gone in. If your child finds it amusing she is much more likely to be motivated to carry on playing.

Children often have a particular activity which they enjoy and which you can use in a variety of ways to teach different skills. Later, once the skill is reasonably established, it can be more easily extended to other activities which are perhaps less interesting. For example, if your child likes games where things move and happen, you could try playing with a marble run which has different coloured pieces. These can be put together and used in a number of ways:

- practice at putting marbles in the run (since marbles are quite small this is good for children's fine motor skills)
- practice at building and fitting things together (one child had no interest in Duplo and other building materials but the marble run element provided the motivation)

- turn-taking (take turns at putting the marbles in or building the run)

- practice at colours – matching ('give me a piece like this'), colour selecting ('give me a blue one') and colour naming ('what colour is this?'), number practice ('give me one piece', 'give me two pieces')

- language (building 'up', marbles going 'in', marbles coming 'out').

How to praise and encourage

Children with special needs often need a lot of exaggerated praise and encouragement because they may not readily pick up on adult pleasure and approval.

Praise has to be exaggerated and over the top. When a child does something particularly good for the first time, give lots of praise (spoken and signed) with big smiles, laughter and clapping to reinforce what you are saying. It can then be toned down as the skill becomes more commonplace.

Children need exaggerated praise and encouragement

When Madeleine first walked from one side of the room to the other the whole family came to admire and praise her to ensure that she realized she had done something good but six months on it is no longer noteworthy.

Children do not necessarily know what they have done which is so good, so you must refer to it when you are praising them. 'Good boy' or 'Good girl' is too abstract. You should say 'Good waving', 'Nice talking', 'Good pooing in the potty' or 'Good sitting still'. Then your child knows which action is the one which has earned the praise. It may sound a bit silly but it is the best way to reinforce their good behaviour.

Try to be positive and encouraging with your child. Get yourself in a mind-set where you look at her attempts in a positive rather than a negative way and concentrate on successes while ignoring failures. If your child tries to put her trousers on and gets both legs in one hole you can say, 'Well done for trying to put your trousers on. Look, this leg goes in this hole,' or you can say 'No, you're doing it all wrong, you've got both legs in the same hole'. One approach is positive and encouraging, the other is demotivating. Children respond much better to the carrot than the stick.

Always give your child the benefit of the doubt if you think she may be attempting a new skill. It can be difficult to be certain that she is attempting something new – it can be so fleeting that it seems just to be a coincidence or a fluke. However, you should always assume that it is deliberate and conscious and therefore reward, praise and encourage your child. If it does turn out to be mere coincidence you haven't lost anything. There is nothing worse than realizing afterwards that you have been ignoring your child's best efforts to practise some new skill.

Rewards

If your child does not find your praise and encouragement sufficiently motivating, you can of course use tangible rewards. Obvious ones are drinks, food and cuddles. Other rewards could be games or activities depending on your child's interests: perhaps a chance to read a book or play with a favourite toy or game.

Rebecca has always liked bubbles and will do most things for the chance to play with them. When beginning potty training, we found them useful as a reward for getting her to sit on the potty. Once there we hoped she would perform so that we could then praise her 'efforts'. It worked and once she had got the idea we abandoned the bubbles quite easily and just kept up the praise.

To use rewards effectively keep them small, immediate and under your control. Use them slightly randomly so that your child sometimes gets one for free and sometimes gets none. This will prevent her getting totally fixated on the reward because you do want her to learn to enjoy the task for its own sake. For example, blow a few bubbles when your child does what you want, occasionally do not blow any, and sometimes blow some for free. You could try a packet of crisps broken into small pieces, hold them behind your back and give them out as and when they are needed. If you give the child the whole packet once she has done something for you, you have lost an opportunity to gain a lot more co-operation. Young children need to see an immediate connection between their behaviour and the reward. They will not understand the promise of a trip to the swings the next day until they are quite 'old'.

With rewards it is worth remembering that:

- you eventually want praise and success at an activity to be enough motivation by themselves and the rewards to be less crucial, otherwise you will be forever bargaining with your child;

- you have to be even-handed in giving out rewards – if you have other children you may not feel it is always appropriate to be rewarding one child and not the others;

- if you use sweets and biscuits as a reward, consider your child's teeth and health.

Rotating and varying toys

Children (and adults) get bored with toys that are around all the time. They may have a toy box full of toys but they cannot find anything to play with. Keep a good half of your toys in the loft or in cupboards and change them round every few months. Keep out the things your child is playing with, making sure you have a variety of toys (for example, not all cars or all posting tins) and put the rest away. When you rotate the toys your child will probably jump on the 'new' toys as if she had never seen them before. Don't worry that you will not have enough toys out. Like the clothes in your cupboard, children only ever seem to play with a relatively small percentage of the toys available.

You can borrow toys relatively cheaply from the toy libraries organized by the National Association of Toy and Leisure Libraries (see p.245). Alternatively you could try exchanging toys with friends.

GENERAL ISSUES FOR CHILDREN WITH SPECIAL NEEDS
Give your child longer to respond than you think she needs

It seems we are programmed as parents to give our children a certain amount of time to respond to us by smiling, talking or playing. When you see mothers cooing to their babies they give them a limited time to coo back before moving on to another activity. There is a remarkable conformity in the time parents allow for a response.[2] However, special needs children can take a lot longer to respond, so parents should consciously allow them longer before turning away. For example, children with cerebral palsy often need a long time to 'process' requests and organize movements like eye pointing or touching objects. When you are playing with your child and want a smile, a noise or a word and have had enough of waiting for a response, count to ten and wait again. Give your child plenty of time. Be patient.

Repetition and perseverance

You will probably find yourself repeating and repeating and repeating words, actions or gestures in order that eventually your child will understand and respond. There is no substitute for

---

2   See Cunningham, C. *et al.* (1981) 'Behavioural and linguistic developments in the interaction of normal and retarded children with their mothers.' *Child Development 52*, 62–70. See also Jones, O.H.M. (1977) 'Mother–child communication with pre-linguistic Down Syndrome and normal infants.' In H.R. Schaffer (ed) *Studies in Mother–Infant Interaction.* London: Academic Press.

repetition even though you may feel as if you are banging your head against a brick wall.

> For years with Jack we repeated simple words – mummy, daddy, bath-time, drink etc. at appropriate moments, practised putting in and on, played peek-a-boo with a cloth all with absolutely no response. Then eventually we did get a response – a passive understanding and then an active involvement and it was all worthwhile.

> Looking back, the things we did with mind-numbing repetitiveness are beginning to pay off now. Right from the start we would talk to Natasha at every opportunity. 'Show me your foot. Yes there's your foot.' I would point. Every day. Now Natasha lifts her foot right up to her head without prompting and points to my foot, her shoe, my shoe and everybody else's shoes.

Give your child plenty of time to respond

Lack of response

One of the hardest things to cope with as a parent is the lack of response that children with special needs often display. It is very draining to be constantly giving your child love, attention, time and care and feel that she is giving nothing back. There is little you can do except persevere and love your child. You will be rewarded even if it is only in a small way.

See Chapter 8, pages 186–189, for ideas on how to get a response from your child and Chapter 1, pages 16–17, on strategies for coping with the stresses and strains of having a child with special needs.

Adopt a multi-sensory approach

Most children with special needs will benefit from a multi-sensory approach. It is clearly vital for those with a sensory impairment but is equally beneficial for those with poor communication skills. Remember the phrase 'Hear, see, do'. Rather than just talk about an object, try to engage the other senses at the same time. So if you are talking about fruits, handle them, feel and touch them, smell them, shake them and taste them too. Your child is much more likely to understand you than if you just point out a picture in a book. Some children pick things up much better visually than verbally. So if you are showing your child something rather than just getting her to watch you or merely telling her what you are doing, try guiding her hands with your hands so that they are actually doing the action (hand-over-hand method).

Even as adults we often find that when someone gives us instructions verbally we think we have understood them but when we come to repeat them we cannot remember a thing. They are much more likely to stick if we have seen them, practised them, written them down, repeated them or found some other way of fixing them in our mind.

Routines and predictability

Children thrive on routines and structure in their lives because they enable them to understand what is going on around them and to recognize and eventually predict situations, creating a feeling of understanding and security.

If your child has a communication problem or a sensory impairment, she may find it difficult to pick up on what is going on and make sense of it. It is therefore even more important that you stick to the same basic routine each day. Keep the environment the same; for example, don't keep changing the furniture around if your child has a visual impairment. Make sure that you are consistent in your response to your child's behaviour, particularly bad behaviour. Children have to go out into the world where so much is unknown and try to make sense of it all. It is a lot easier if they have learnt that their own home environment is governed by a kind of timetable (e.g. getting up and going to bed at certain times, having regular meals) and by social manners (e.g. sitting down to eat and drink). However, routine does not mean rigidity, for instance bedtime does not necessarily have to be on the dot of 7.00 but it should be between 6.30 and 7.30, say, and not between 7.00 and 10.00. Also some children get fixated on routines and so need some variation within the routine to prevent fixations from occurring.

The importance of generalizing skills

In order to say that a child has achieved a certain skill, she has to demonstrate that she can do it not just with familiar toys but with unknown objects, in all sorts of circumstances and for a variety of people. Professionals, in particular, always want evidence that a skill has been generalized in this way. For example, in order to say that a child can match pictures, she has to demonstrate this skill with any set of pictures – not just the ones she has been using at home. If she can do it with one set, she will certainly learn to do it with others, but she has to be given the opportunity.

Give your child lots of opportunities to use different materials in a variety of situations when playing so that she can learn to experiment and explore and expand her knowledge and understanding.

Don't get fixated on one skill

It is easy to get fixated on teaching your child one particular skill as if it will transform her life. It might be because of what people say to you – 'Is she sitting up yet?' or 'Is she walking?' – or because of your views of what is important. However, it is not usually helpful to have such a fixation. First, parents may then ignore all the other skills which are developing simultaneously and need to be recognized and encouraged. Second, it ignores the way children develop, which is as a whole. It is difficult to isolate one particular skill because skills develop in an inter-related and complicated way. For example, when a child puts an object in a box she needs the physical skill to grasp and release it and the intellectual skill to see the relationship between the sizes of the container and the object.

Equally, learning a new skill in one area will have a profound and beneficial effect on others where a connection is not necessarily immediately obvious. For example, an improvement in communication skills will mean a child has a greater understanding of social situations and how to behave. Learning to sit up will enable a child to handle toys better, explore them more, see what's going on around her and learn from that and, surprisingly, make a greater range of sounds.

Completing tasks

If you ask your child to do something and she does not want to or cannot do it then you should complete the task yourself saying perhaps, 'Mummy put the piece in then'. The point is that you want your child to feel that it is important that she completes an activity or game. If you ask her to do something and she does not do it so that you merely shrug and put it aside she will form the impression that it does not matter whether or not she does it and will be less likely to co-operate in the future.

STAY IN TUNE WITH YOUR CHILD

There is a danger in the way that we look at child development and, indeed, in the very nature of this book that parents become too focused on skill development, on the next stage and on comparisons with peers.

As well as striving for progress as you see it, enjoy your child and follow her in her play, in her language and in her activities. Copy her. Go along with her. Enter her world and respect and learn what she is about. If you are doing something with your child and she does something unexpected do not necessarily correct her, go along with it and see what happens. Empathize

Follow your child in her play

with your child. See things from her point of view rather than always be trying to get her to conform to your own world and expectations.

HIGH EXPECTATIONS

Have high expectations of what your child will achieve and don't impose barriers on her by saying she will never sit up or communicate, because she may do. Work towards her achieving all skills and fulfilling her potential. You will then give your child the opportunities, the respect and the environment she needs to develop. You may have to modify your expectations in the light of experience but it is best to aim for the top and fall short, knowing that you have done everything you can.

If you assume that your child is capable of achieving very little, she will achieve very little because such an attitude is self-fulfilling. You can feel that you're being very hard forcing your child to do physical exercises or play games that she clearly does not enjoy but often she will gradually start to enjoy them as they become familiar and easier. If in the end it means she becomes more independent, the benefit will be all hers.

Concentrate on small steps at a time. Give everything your best effort and demand that she does the same.

My sister and I had our babies close together. Her little boy was bringing back paintings from playgroup by the age of two. 'My Natasha will never do that,' I thought negatively. 'She can't even sit up and she's nearly two.' Natasha is now three and a half. She not only sits up but is beginning to bear weight and her favourite subject at Nursery is ... painting! She also bakes cakes for me and is learning to play with sand. I am more patient now and certainly more optimistic.

CHAPTER 3

Cognitive Development

What are cognitive skills?

By exploring and experimenting with objects and their environment, children gain an understanding of how things work; they learn what the properties and capabilities of objects and materials are and they discover that they can affect and influence what happens around them. The cognitive skills which children acquire in pre-school years underlie later development in reading, writing and mathematics as well as conceptual and logical thought.

Chronological development

Newborn baby

A newborn baby is primarily interested in people and faces. Given different things to look at a newborn or very young baby will choose to look at a face. A real face is the most interesting but babies are also attracted by pictures of faces, even if they are crudely drawn, imaginary or even grotesque.

Copying

Babies copy adults from a very young age, for example by making faces or by sticking out their tongues. Copying is a crucial skill because it is by copying adults and other children that children learn to do new things and to say new words. It therefore underlies all development and is fundamental to learning cognitive skills.

Exploring objects

It is only after spending a long time observing faces and people that children become interested in exploring objects. Initially they take everything to their mouth because the mouth is the most sensitive part of the body and will therefore give them the most information about each object. Then they start to shake objects, to hit them against other surfaces, to examine them, feel them, drop and throw them. Using all their senses in this way children learn about the properties of each object – its feel and texture, whether it is hard or soft, heavy or light, the noise it makes, whether it tastes good, whether it changes shape or stays rigid and what it looks like from all angles.

Object permanence

Children initially think that objects and people only exist when they can see them and that as soon as they have disappeared from sight they no longer exist. Consequently, a young child will cry when his mother leaves the room because he thinks she has vanished. He will not look for a toy that has rolled out of sight because, as far as he is concerned, it does not exist.[1]

Gaining an understanding that objects continue to exist even when they cannot be seen is a major development milestone, indicating that children have started to develop the ability to conceptualize. As a result of this particular understanding, they will start to look for things, accept absences and remember people, toys and actions instead of believing everything is new each time it appears. When children start dropping toys out of their pram or highchair and see their mothers returning them over and over again they start to get the idea of object permanence. They then watch to see where the toys go and to look for them. They learn to find partially covered toys and later wholly covered toys. They play peek-a-boo using a cloth because they know someone is still there even if hidden.

1   See Piaget, J. (1953) *The Origins of Intelligence in the Child.* London: Routledge and Kegan Paul. For a summary of Piaget's work on child development see Sime, M. (1980) *Read Your Child's Thoughts: Pre-School Learning Piaget's Way.* London: Thames and Hudson.

Exploring the environment

Once mobile, children want to explore their environment and find out about everything around them. They go through a phase of not being content with the box of toys in the middle of the carpet. They want to open and close all the doors, empty the cupboards and reach the precious ornaments on the top shelf. This is as important as exploring objects because through it children widen their understanding of their environment. They explore how things like doors work, they learn to examine the same things from different angles and they learn about natural phenomena like light, shade and echoes.

Cause and effect

Once children start playing with objects they learn that if they hit a rattle against a hard surface they will get a certain noise or that if they squeeze a certain ball they will hear a squeak. This is the start of learning about cause and effect. One of the easiest examples to think of is a child pressing a button on a pop-up toy and seeing that the animal jumps up. It takes a little time for him to realize that the animal popping up is a direct consequence of his pressing the button. Children learn all sorts of examples of cause and effect, for instance switching on lights, turning on the television and playing a keyboard.

Learning about cause and effect is a fundamental skill because it gives children the awareness that they can influence the objects and environment around them and that they live in a world which is, to an extent, controlled and controllable.

Relational play

After mouthing, shaking and hitting objects, children go on to test how objects can be used in relation to others. For example they put a spoon in a cup, a brick in a box, a ball under a stool, or fill up and empty containers. They are beginning to make comparisons between objects; for example, that 'this block is too big and will not go in' or 'that block has to be placed centrally otherwise it will fall off the top of the tower'. These kinds of comparisons about size, weight and placement are the start of mathematical thinking and the basis of conceptual thought.

Building

As children play with more than one object and see how they can be combined, they start to build. Initially they build simple towers with large blocks and enjoy knocking them down. Then, as their fine motor skills improve, they learn to use smaller, fiddlier pieces and build taller towers as well as bridges and other constructions using bricks, Duplo, train tracks and other construction materials. They are learning about weight, shapes, three-dimensional objects and size.

Matching, selecting and naming

When learning a new concept children always learn in the order of: match, select, name. First they see that two objects are the same or share similar qualities (matching), then they have a passive understanding (responding to being asked to select) and finally they are able to actively name the object.

Matching

Children first learn to match objects which are identical, e.g. this ball is the same as that ball and not that car. They start with actual objects like bricks or teddies, then they learn to match pictures of objects to the real thing and then to other pictures. Later they are able to match colours, then such concepts as big and little, long and short.

The ability to match, in other words to recognize similarities and differences, is a crucial skill for later mathematics and reading.

Selecting

Having learnt to match objects, children go on to select them. For example, a father asks his child to give him the picture of the train or the blue brick, where there is a choice of several pictures or objects. When selecting, the child has to recognize and respond to the name but not to actively use it.

Naming

The final stage is for children to be able to name the object, picture or colour. So when shown a picture of a car, the child says 'car'. This requires him to recall the name accurately.

Sorting and grouping

Children learn to examine a set of objects and sort them into groups consisting of the same or similar things. For instance, when tidying up a child might sort his toys into a pile of Duplo and a pile of train track, or blue Lego and yellow Lego.

Later on they classify and group by a common factor, for instance putting all the cooking things or all the bathroom things together. This is a skill which we continue to use later in life to organize our possessions and environments, create order and aid thought processes and memory.

Pre-numeracy skills

Children repeat numbers by rote from quite an early age but do not actually understand the concepts behind numbers for a long time. They have to learn that one means one thing, two means two things and so on (the so-called 'oneness of one'). They first learn 'one' and 'two', then 'lots/more' before learning further numbers.

Children also learn simple concepts which underlie mathematics such as big and small, long and short, heavy and light, and the language of maths – capacity, weight, measure, big, bigger and biggest.

Pre-reading skills

Children develop an understanding that writing conveys meaning, can be read and is the same every time it is read. They gain this by looking at books. They first look at picture books and are generally interested in the pictures. They then start to point to specific pictures and later to listen to simple stories which are read to them. After they have understood that pictures can convey meaning, they begin to realize that writing also has meaning, can be read and is understood. They learn that it is read the same every time. So when they look at familiar books which have often been read to them, they start to predict what is going to happen and fill in missing words from memory. Children sometimes get cross if you don't read it the same way each time.

The other component is an ability to match and remember the shapes of letters. Children first learn to match and recognize pictures and then move on to match symbols and finally letters. The first words they recognize are the most familiar ones such as their own names and those of family members which they see on labels, notes, cards, signs and in books.

Pre-writing skills

Drawing and writing are complex skills which marry a physical skill with a cognitive understanding. To draw, a child not only needs the physical control and skill to make a mark, but he also needs to understand the relationship between the pen and the paper and to understand the idea that a mark can represent something.

Initially children just scribble randomly before becoming aware of the marks they are actually making. Then they consciously draw vertical then horizontal lines, dots then circles. They begin to control their movements and look at what they are doing and understand that they can control their marks. The usual sequence of marks is shown in the illustration below.

The first marks a child makes

They learn that making marks has two purposes: to make shapes like a cross, triangle or square which can be made into pictures or alternatively to make letters such as A, B and C which can be used for communication. They start to copy simple symbols such as X, +, O, V, H and T and draw simple pictures of people and houses.

Parallel development
Memory

Babies can probably remember some things from birth because early on they remember the sound of their mother's voice and can recognize her face and smell. Children pick up on 'cues' which remind them of what is going to happen; for example, they remember that the sound of a tap running indicates a bath. As they grow up their memory develops so that experiences and objects are remembered and do not seem new each time. They remember who people are, what things do and how to perform certain actions.

Once the idea of object permanence is fully established, memory will develop gradually. Children first remember people and objects in context though they can often be thrown by meeting someone out of context: for instance, if a child sees his grandmother in his playgroup rather than in her home it may take time to work out who she is. Later, childen remember routines and incidents which had a particular impact on them.

Developing memory skills is vital not only for cognitive skills such as reading and writing but also for language skills.

Attention span

Children have very short attention spans and are easily distracted. They flit from one activity to another as they hear interesting noises, see different toys or as people move around them. They learn over time to block out other distractions and to continue with their own activities regardless of what is going on around them. For a period they become so intent on their activities that they are difficult to distract. Later on, they develop the ability to respond to different inputs at the same time, for example they can handle verbal instructions in the middle of playing a game.[2]

Concept of time

At first children only have a concept of 'here and now' and they want all their needs and demands met instantly. They do, however, develop an understanding of a sequence of actions – 'we will go to the shops and then we will go to the playground' –

2   Cooper, J., Moodley, M. and Reynell, J. (1978) *Helping Language Development.* London: Arnold.

and of before and after. They learn the concepts of present, future and past time in that order, i.e. today, then tomorrow and finally yesterday.

Imaginative play

Imaginative play is when children go beyond using toys or objects for the purpose they were intended and introduce ideas into their play which come from their imagination. Although there are lots of different academic theories on the purpose of imaginative play, it is clear that it has a very important place in child development. It is a useful way for children to practise their skills without fear of failure. They can try out new ideas and develop their understanding of the world, of social situations and of human relationships (hence the use of play therapy for children who have been abused). By playing imaginatively, children also develop the ability to think abstractly – this box is a boat and this stick an oar – which is important for language development and for later cognitive skills. They also use it to practise talking. How often do parents hear their own words being used by children pretending to tell a naughty teddy off, or admonishing a pretend husband for being late home from work?

Imaginative play

Children start by exploring the properties of toys. Given a toy car, a child at a very early stage of development will put it in its mouth, bang it on the floor, shake it etc. Later the child understands the function of a toy and plays with it appropriately; for example, pushing the toy car along the ground. He demonstrates imaginative play when he gets two toy cars and bashes them together saying 'crash'.

Genuine imaginative play is initiated by the child and should not be confused with play which is initiated by an adult. For instance, an adult might run the car along a track and the child might copy him or an adult might suggest that he fills the car up with some pretend petrol and he obeys. The child is not demonstrating imaginative play, just the ability to copy and understand verbal instructions.

Imaginative play takes all sorts of forms. Children play using a small element of make-believe like drinking from an empty cup, or they act out roles that they have seen others perform, like a postman or a shopkeeper. Alternatively, they substitute one object for another, for example, pretending a stick is an aeroplane or a string of beads is a caterpillar, or using Duplo and other building materials to create houses, cars or people.

GAMES AND ACTIVITIES

General guidelines

Give your child lots of opportunities to experiment, explore and be creative with toys and objects whatever his stage of development. He will need to practise what he has learnt on as many different materials as possible and in lots of different environments so that he really understands what he is doing and why things are happening. For example, build towers with wooden bricks, beakers, barrels, soft bricks, tins of tomatoes, Tupperware boxes etc. Do it in the sitting room with bricks, in the bath with sponges and in the garden with flowerpots.

Allow your child to play with things the wrong way as well as the right way, because that is how he will learn. If he tries to dig sand with the wrong end of the spade let him see what happens rather than insisting that he turns the spade round. Don't over-organize him.

Chronological development
Copying

It is impossible to make a child copy you if he does not want to or does not see the point. You have to start by copying him and then, as he sees the fun of it, he will start to copy you back. Copy any noises he makes like coos or raspberries. Copy any gestures he makes or any facial expressions like smiles or grimaces. If he shakes a rattle, puts bricks in a bucket or throws a toy, copy that or indeed any other spontaneous play he performs. Copy repeatedly. You will not know whether or not you are having any success until one day you find your child copying you.

> One Christmas when the extended family was together we all copied Charlotte lifting her arms up high at meal-times. She found the sight of all these adults copying her so funny that she did it endlessly to get us to copy her. It was a major breakthrough.

Copying gestures

There are many good rhymes to use when getting your child to copy gestures, some examples are:

> If you're happy and you know it, clap your hands
> If you're happy and you know it, clap your hands
> If you're happy and you know it, and you really want to show it
> If you're happy and you know it, clap your hands.

Other verses:
... touch your nose/toes/ knees/head
... give a smile
... say 'we are'
... stamp your feet

Pat-a-cake, pat-a-cake, baker's man
Bake me a cake as fast as you can
Pat it and prick it and mark it with B
And bake it in the oven for baby and me.

Wind the bobbin up, wind the bobbin up
Pull pull clap clap clap
Point to the ceiling, point to the floor
Point to the window, point to the door
Clap your hands together one, two, three
Put your hands upon your knee.

The wheels on the bus go round and round, round and round, round
and round
The wheels on the bus go round and round, all day long.

Other verses:
The bell on the bus goes ding ding ding...
The wipers on the bus go swish swish swish...
The horn on the bus goes beep beep beep...
The children on the bus go up and down...
The ladies on the bus go knit, knit, knit...

Here we go round the mulberry bush, the mulberry bush, the
mulberry bush
Here we go round the mulberry bush, on a cold and frosty morning.

Other verses:
This is the way we brush our teeth, brush our teeth, brush our
teeth...
This is the way we comb our hair...
This is the way we stamp our feet...
This is the way we clap our hands...
This is the way we wash our face...
This is the way we wave goodbye...

I'm a little teapot, short and stout
Here's my handle, here's my spout
When you see the tea cups hear me shout
Tip me up and pour me out.

One potato, two potato, three potato, four
Five potato, six potato, seven potato, more
Bang one fist on the other.

Open, shut them, open, shut them, give a little clap
Open, shut them, open, shut them, put them in your lap
Creep them, creep them, up to your little chin
Open wide your little mouth, but do not put them in.
Use your hands in the rhyme, opening and clenching your fist.

- Perform a simple version of Simon Says where your child copies your gestures. For example, 'Simon says put your hands on your head' or 'Simon says smile'.

- Watch nursery-rhyme videos with your child and perform the actions with him.

- Children often prefer 'real activities' to mock ones so household chores are a good way of getting your child to copy you. If you are doing the dusting give him a duster, similarly give him a cloth when wiping the table. Offer him the dustpan and brush to help you sweep the floor. Get him to help empty the washing basket and load the washing machine.

- Look in a mirror, make faces and noises and see if your child will copy you.

- Try the hand-over-hand method to get your child to copy actions. Begin by guiding your child's hands to, say, pick up a brick and put it in a box. After a number of goes, as you feel him beginning to co-operate, move your hands up to his wrists. As you feel he knows what he is expected to do, move your hands up to his elbows so that you are giving less of a prompt. Eventually he may require merely a touch on the arm before being able to complete the action alone.

Other ideas are also listed in Chapter 4, page 100.

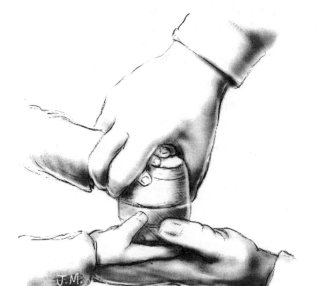

Hand-over-hand method

Exploring objects

Children need lots of opportunities to explore and experiment with as many different types of objects as they can safely use. If your child has access to a variety of things you may touch upon something which he finds particularly stimulating or interesting. You will also give him the chance to generalize his skills, make comparisons and develop his understanding.

- Do not be restricted to toys from the toy box but find objects which have different and interesting textures, shapes, colours and qualities which your child can explore and examine.
- Look around the house for everyday objects, bits of packaging, kitchen utensils, different fabrics and materials.
- Make up rattles by filling containers with rice, pasta and pulses or plastic bottles with coloured pegs, marbles, coins or water.
- Put Velcro hair rollers on a piece of felt. They make a lovely noise when pulled off.

- Let your child play with toys with different textures. You can buy some toys which incorporate different textures or make up a box or tray of objects with different qualities – sandpaper, fabrics (velvet, leather, fun fur, hessian), bubble wrap, metal, wax, wood, paper.

- Find toys with lights and sounds as they appeal to most children.

- Use toys which are easy for your child to handle initially then gradually reduce the size.

- Play with any of the objects or toys listed in Chapter 6, pages 158–160.

Picking up on cues

- Give your child as many cues as possible so that he knows what is about to happen and can therefore start to recognize a routine and make sense of the world around him.

- Warn him of what is going to happen in simple language, preferably using the same words each time.

- Use non-verbal cues: for example, place him in the bathroom so he can hear the water running for his bath; get the plastic bags out each time you go shopping or rattle cutlery noisily to signify a meal.

- You could play some music a few minutes before the end of an activity to signal that it's time to clear up.

Object permanence

- Play hide and seek with a favourite toy or teddy. To begin with partially hide the toy under a cloth and ask 'Where's the teddy?' and then reveal it for your child. See if your child will find it. Once he does find it, make it harder by gradually covering more of the toy until it is totally covered.

- Hide toys under pots, beakers or containers and then reveal them or get your child to find them. Use clear pots to begin with and then coloured ones.

- When your child is in a high chair, hold a noisy toy (e.g. a rattle, bell or squeaky toy) under the tray and move it from one side to the other. Get your child to follow the noise and then pop it up every now and again to show him. Eventually he will reach for it.

- If your child starts throwing things out of his pram or highchair, keep bringing them back to show him so that he gets the idea that they continue to exist even if he cannot see them.

- Roll marbles, cars or balls down tubes and show your child that they exist, disappear from sight and reappear at the other end.

- Play at crawling through tunnels, disappearing from sight and then reappearing.

- Play lots of peek-a-boo games with your child using a cloth or your hands to hide your face. See also Chapter 4, page 95 for more ideas.

- If your child has a visual impairment, place toys slightly out of reach and get your child to search for them so that he gradually realizes that they are still there even though he cannot touch them.

Exploring the environment

Children need to have the opportunity to explore different and unusual environments. When children become mobile they are able to turn themselves in their cot or manoeuvre themselves into different places so that they can experience the echoes under the table and behind the sofa, feel the textures of different flooring materials, the smells in various rooms, the patterns of light and shade under a tree or a shadow passing. If your child is not mobile he may need help to experience these things.

Put your child in a variety of places, e.g. in different parts of the room — under the window, under the table, in the corner — rather than just on a rug in the middle. Vary sleeping positions and the location of the highchair at meal times. Take him around the house with you, as you move about to give him the opportunity to experience different rooms.

Cause and effect

If your child combines a lack of understanding of cause and effect with poor physical skills make sure you use toys which require a very light touch. Many commercial pop-up toys are quite stiff. Try the following ideas of toys and games which show cause and effect.

- pop-up toys with buttons to press, slide and turn;
- toys with buttons which produce lights and music;
- jack-in-the-boxes;
- holographic paper – put on knobs and buttons to stimulate interest in pushing and pressing;
- books with buttons to press for flashing lights or noises or both;
- books with flaps;
- keyboards and children's tape recorders;
- children's computer games;
- if your child has a visual impairment, try to use toys with switches and lights.

A little bit extreme but it worked: we painted one of the memory buttons on the telephone with red nail polish and Natasha now pushes the button and phones Grandma!

Relational play

Children learn how one object relates to another by having lots of opportunities to play with different things. They then learn to judge the relative size and weight of objects.

Placing one object on another

Get your child to place a smallish object on top of a large one and knock it down with a lot of noise and excitement. Then introduce all sorts of different objects so that the child learns to place the object directly on top and not on the edge, and to use big blocks and beakers at the bottom and smaller ones at the top.

Placing one object in another

- Use small, easily handled objects and a large shallow container like a cake tin. When the object goes in move the tin around so your child hears a nice rattling noise. Then introduce smaller containers with smaller openings. Encourage your child to move objects from one container to another.
- Use posting boxes with different shapes. If posting is difficult use tins which have soft plastic tops like marmelade, coffee or formula milk tins. Cut a hole in the top for a ping-pong ball or other small object.

Placing one object on another

Rolling and sliding

Get your child to roll marbles, cars and balls down slopes, slides and tubes. Put any flat surface on an angle – a book, a tray, a piece of wood and roll something down it. Likewise use a tube from a roll of wrapping paper or kitchen towel. Increase and decrease the angle of the slope to speed the ball up or slow it down.

Moving objects without touching them

- Line bricks up on the floor and shunt them along by pushing the last brick with another. You can use two cars to achieve the same effect.

- Encourage your child to pull cars and animals towards him by pulling on their leads rather than pulling the objects themselves. Attach a string to a favourite toy and pull it along.

- Place a drink out of reach on a piece of paper and draw the paper towards you to show your child how you can bring it within reach.

Building

- Develop the ideas in 'placing one object on another' above by using more complex materials like Duplo, Stickle Bricks, blocks of different shapes – cylinders, rectangles as well as squares.

- Rather than just building towers, build other shapes like walls, bridges and houses.
- Put train tracks together to make different layouts

Matching, selecting and naming

Children start matching real objects and then move on to pictures and then more abstract concepts like colour and size. It is important for children to be able to spot very tiny similarities and differences for later maths and reading skills. Think how similar an 'e' and a 'c' are.

Matching real objects

Start off with two sets of three simple everyday objects. Place one set in front of your child and then give him the other set, one by one, and get him to place each one alongside its pair. For instance, lay out an apple, spoon and brick in front of your child. As an example place the second spoon alongside the first. Then give

Matching real objects

him the apple and see if he will do the same and then finally the brick. Change the objects as he progresses.

Matching pictures

In the same way, match two sets of simple pictures. Start off with a choice of three clear pictures of everyday objects and get your child to place the identical one on top. Then try more complicated pictures and more of them. Progress to very simple line drawing sketches. Use snap or lotto cards or pictures from the same book. Later you can draw your own simple sketches.

Matching shapes

Get your child to match shapes by learning to put the ball in the round hole and the cube in the square hole. Use simple posting boxes or wooden form board puzzles to match shapes like circles, squares, triangles and ovals. Initially a child will succeed by trial and error trying each hole in turn until one goes in and will need a lot of help. Gradually he will learn to recognize shapes starting usually with the circle and then identifying squares, triangles and stars.

Matching symbols

Instead of matching pictures draw simple symbols on paper and get your child to match them; for example, a circle, cross and star.

Matching colours

Begin with the colours red and yellow which are the easiest and then move on to blue and green. Then you can introduce others.

Start by having a yellow and red bag, bucket or basket and go round the house gathering red or yellow objects and toys to put in the bags. Net bags for holding lemons and oranges are very good for this.

Try different games to get your child to match colours – build red or yellow towers, have red and yellow pieces of paper or bricks and buckets and put the relevant colours in each, match the colours in a child's tea set, thread beads of the right colour.

Matching sizes

Start with big and little and make the difference in size very obvious. Use saucepans, spoons and Tupperware containers.

Selecting and naming

Once your child is matching successfully, ask him to select the object of your choice from a group of objects. For example, have a toy car, a book and a cup in front of your child and ask him to give you the cup. Do the same with pictures, colours, shapes and sizes. Play shopping using different objects.

Finally, once your child is selecting well, ask him to name the objects, pictures, shapes etc.

Sorting toys

Sorting and grouping

Get your child to:

- Sort toys when you are tidying up so that, for example, Duplo goes in one box and books in another.
- Sort knives, forks and spoons after washing up, clean clothes for members of the family or buttons and beads.
- Sort similar things to make your child look carefully, for example different-shaped shells, leaves or jigsaw-puzzle pieces.

- Move on to pairing objects which go together using real objects or pictures, for example cup and saucer, knife and fork, socks and shoes and hat and scarf.

- Group objects or pictures of objects which are used for the same purpose, for instance sort cooking utensils from bath things or toys from clothes.

Pre-numeracy skills

Sequencing

The following games encourage children to recognize and repeat patterns as these are very important for mathematics.

Using beads or bricks, start with easy patterns using just two colours, then introduce more colours and later variations in size. Get your child to match a pattern you have made with beads, buttons or bricks using colour, size and shape. Then ask him to continue the pattern on.

One-to-one matching

Get your child to:

- Lay the table for dinner so your child places one fork with one knife or a spoon in a bowl for each person. Lay the table for a teddy bear's tea party.

One-to-one matching

- Draw a picture where your child has to connect one object with another, for example a knife and fork, a dog and his lunch, animals and their young.
- Share out things like toys or food at meal-times. 'One for Robert, one for Peter…'
- Place one of four objects in each of four containers, for example, a spoon in a cup or a ball in a bowl.

Understanding the 'oneness of one'

Count things but make them tangible and physical. Handle the objects as you count them – one brick, two bricks. Start with one and two. Use things that your child can handle like bricks, balls, marbles, shoes, socks or biscuits.

When you are doing something, ask your child to give you one or two objects. For example, if you are playing with Duplo, ask him to give you two pieces, then one piece, then two pieces and so on.

Understanding shape and size

Play games to emphasize concepts such as large and small, long and short, light and heavy, lots and a few, and full and empty. Water and sand (wet and dry) are good for many of these concepts. There are also lots of books available which illustrate these concepts well.

Counting rhymes

Sing all sorts of counting rhymes to establish the sequence of numbers, for example:

> One two, buckle my shoe,
> Three four, knock on my door
> Five six, pick up sticks
> Seven eight, lay them straight
> Nine ten, big fat hen.

> Five fat sausages sizzling in a pan
> One went pop and then it went bang.
> Four fat sausages…

> Five little monkeys jumping on the bed
> One fell off and bumped his head
> Mummy called the doctor and this is what he said

'No more monkeys jumping on the bed'.
Four little monkeys etc.

One two three four five
Once I caught a fish alive
Six seven eight nine ten
Then I let it go again
Why did you let it go
Because it bit my finger so
Which finger did it bite
This little finger on the right.

Ten green bottles hanging on the wall
Ten green bottles hanging on the wall
And if one green bottle should accidentally fall
There'd be nine green bottles hanging on the wall.

One man went to mow, went to mow a meadow
One man and his dog went to mow a meadow
Two men went to mow, went...

This old man, he played one, he played nick nack on my drum
With a nick nack paddywack give the dog a bone
This old man went rolling home.

> *Other verses:*
> This old man he played two, he played...
> Two – shoe
> Three – tree
> Four – door
> Five – hive
> Six – on his sticks
> Seven – up in heaven
> Eight – gate
> Nine – line
> Ten – hen

One potato, two potato, three potato, four
Five potato, six potato, seven potato more.

Five currant buns in the baker's shop
Big and round, with a cherry on the top
Along came a boy with a penny in his hand

He bought one bun and took it right away.
Four currant buns in the baker's...

Pre-reading skills

Above all, children need to develop an interest in books. Spend
time together enjoying books. First of all look at bright, bold and

Developing an enjoyment of books

simple picture books of familiar objects, animals and people.
Children have to learn to hold books the right way round and to
'read' them from left to right.

Then move on to very simple story books where people are
performing actions – for example a day's routine or a shopping
trip – so that he gets the idea of a sequence of events.

- Get your child to find a particular picture in a book or a
  specific book.

- Encourage your child to interact with the book, for example
  by pretending to eat the food in the picture, kiss the doll, cut
  the cake with a knife or pat the dog.

- Children need to learn that writing means something. Try to show that you can read the words in books, in cards, on signs and on shopping lists.

- Rhymes and rhythms all help children's language and reading skills so sing and say lots of nursery rhymes and songs. Get your child to fill in words or to predict what is going to happen next.

- Find 'spot the difference' puzzles where your child has to point out the differences between a set of two pictures.

All the matching skills mentioned above on pages 66–67 are vital. Children need to have quite detailed visual discrimination to differentiate between letters. Once children can match symbols you can start getting them to match letters, numbers and words.

- Write out two words like 'car' and 'television' on cards and get your child to match another card saying 'television'.

- Put names on bedroom doors, by place mats and on pegs so that your child sees them around the house. His own name and those of his family will probably be the first words he recognizes.

- Create a photograph album with pictures of family members and write their names next to them. Play matching games. Write out the names on individual cards. First get your child to match the word to the word and picture. Then cover up the picture and match it just to the word. Finally get your child to match the word to the picture only.

- Stick the names of objects on the objects themselves and play a matching or fetching game. For example, stick the words 'door', 'television', 'chair' and 'teddy' on the relevant object and give your child a second sticker which he has to place with the first sticker. Alternatively, get him to bring you the matching sticker. 'Post-it' notes are good for this.

Because developing memory is also vital for pre-reading skills, play the games given below in the section on Memory, pages 75–76.

Pre-writing skills

Once your child is making marks on paper, play games which encourage greater accuracy and the idea of tracing figures on paper.

- Play with road-map floor-mats and encourage your child to trace the journey of the car or with train sets where children push the train along the track.

- Get your child to play with toys which have beads threaded onto wires and where he moves the beads along the wires to get them to the other end.

- Make patterns in sand and encourage your child to copy you.

- Draw two pictures on a piece of paper – for example, two shoes, a dog to his dinner, patches of colour, letters or numbers. Get your child to join them with a line.

- Encourage your child to draw lines going up and down or across the page.

- Draw two parallel lines across the page about an inch or two apart and see if your child will draw lines from left to right within the lines.

- Draw wide lines in a fluorescent pen and get your child to trace the lines with his pencil. Make the lines wide and straight initially then narrower, with curves, zigzags and ultimately quite complex.

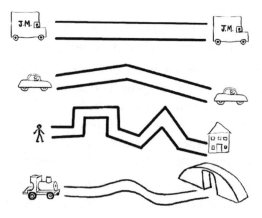

Draw the journey

- Draw two cars and a wide road linking them. Get your child to draw the journey following the road. At first make the road straight, then with angular bends, and finally curvy.

- Get your child to copy simple figures like a circle, cross and T or to trace over them.

Colouring

Initially, children colour the whole piece of paper, but you gradually want them to gain the control to colour smaller and more specific sections.

Start by getting your child to colour in a large piece of paper and then give him a smaller piece. Try placing the paper on a piece of black card so that he keeps the marks to the paper. Then introduce easy pictures for him to colour in, for instance an outline of a circle, car, train or person. Make the edge very thick and the picture a reasonable size but not fiddly so your child does not get bored too quickly. Then reduce the size of the picture and get your child to colour within its boundaries.

You could try raising the edge of the picture so that he cannot go over the edge of it (this is particularly useful if your child is visually impaired). Glue some string around the edge of the picture or use glue that dries in a solid raised line.

Look under Chapter 5, pages 150–151, for further ideas for games.

Parallel development
Memory

- Read a very simple story to your child a few times and ask him to tell you what happens next.

- Singing nursery rhymes and action songs is a good way of improving memory as children will fill in the last word or remember some of the key words. If they are not talking they may be able to show that they remember what happens by using the action or sign.

- Ask your child to tell you what has happened during the day or talk to him about what has happened.

- Ask your child to get things out or to put things away in the correct place.

- Play pairs with cards. Place pairs of cards face down and get each player to turn over two cards. If they are a pair, the player can remove them, if not they are replaced.

- Play a version of lotto, by placing the cards face down in front of you and turning a card over in turn. If you turn one over which fits on your board you can pick it up and the first person to complete his board wins.

- Try a very simple version of the traditional party game where you place two or three objects on a tray, handle them and name them. Then cover them up and ask your child to name them or, alternatively, take something away and ask your child what is missing.

Extending attention spans

Don't be unrealistic in your expectations. All small children have a short attention span which develops over time.

Finish all activities, even if it means you complete a game very quickly, to give the idea that your child should work through his activities to the end.

Remove distractions as far as possible (see Chapter 2 pp.32–34).

Don't make activities too difficult but do make them fun so that your child will want to do them and will not be frustrated by his lack of ability.

Establish appropriate places for doing things – eating at the table, sitting down to paint, etc.

- Play games where your child has to wait for a moment, rather than get immediate satisfaction. For example, say 'ready, steady, go' and '1, 2, 3' and then roll a ball or push a car or knock something down.

- Blow bubbles and make your child wait for a moment before blowing more.

- Find an activity your child enjoys and seek to extend it very gradually, either by continuing the play or by introducing one new element to keep the idea going until just before your child gets bored. For example, if he has a train set start by laying out the track, put the train on, then add a driver, carriages, put things in the carriages, make a bridge, make a station, get the train to stop and change passengers.

- Alternatively, try lots of short activities in quick succession but maintaining concentration.

- Use a book like *Ketchup on your Cornflakes?* by Nick Sharratt (published by Picture Hippos) where you ask lots of questions such as 'Do you like ketchup on your toothbrush?', 'Do you like ketchup on your toes?' and 'Do you like ketchup in your bath?' requiring a 'No' before you reach 'Do you like ketchup on your chips?' 'Yes.'

Concept of time

Children only gradually gain an understanding of the passing of time. However, it is worth trying to help them to understand if only because it can be a source of great frustration and unhappiness when children want to do something 'now' and cannot.

- An understanding of a sequence of events must come first. So in daily life explain the sequence of events. For example, first you are going to tidy up and then you will have lunch. Keep it simple and repeat it frequently.

- Show sequences of actions when reading a book or when playing with dolls and teddies.

- Give a timetable verbally each day, maybe for half a day at a time. 'We are going to have breakfast, then we are going to go and see George and Martha.'

- Point out clocks in books and around the house and talk about it being 'time for drinks', 'time for school'.

Visual timetables

Children who find it difficult to cope with an open-ended situation and like structure in their lives may find it helpful to have timetables with pictures so that they can see how their day is organized and what they are going to do next.

Visual timetables are developed in the TEACCH programme. This is a system used with children with autism and communication disorders.[3] It is detailed and complex but the following shows how it can be used in a simplified way in the home.

3   See note on page 34 for contact details.

Visual timetable: lunch, swings, walk and then shopping

The timetable might cover a whole day with a morning activity, lunch, afternoon activity, tea and bed, or it might cover a few hours only. It should be organized according to the needs of the child.

Put Velcro on a board or strip of card or wood to which you can then attach pictures or objects. The timetable should run from left to right or from top to bottom.

Use objects, photographs, pictures, symbols or words to depict each activity on the timetable.

Below is a list of the different formats you can use from the simplest to the most sophisticated. Choose the form most appropriate to your child's level of understanding.

- Use actual objects to indicate an activity. For example, breakfast could be a spoon, swimming could be an arm band, lunch could be a banana and a shopping trip could be a carrier bag.

- Use clear photographs of actual objects or of your child doing a specific activity. Playgroup could be a photograph of your child at playgroup, a trip to the supermarket could be a photograph of your child in his supermarket trolley, a visit from Granny could be a picture of Granny in your home.

- Use simple line drawings of the activity. Draw a picture of a bowl of Frosties, horse riding or the car.

- Use the Makaton symbols to show the activities. Makaton publish a range of symbols which are clear, stylized, line drawings (see p.106 for examples and p.244 for the Makaton address).

- Finally use words just as anybody would do in a diary.

If the timetable works for your child and you use it over a period of time, move your child on to the next level when he is ready. When you are making the transition from one stage to the next use both methods in conjunction for a period.

Although it may seem very complicated initially, most children in fact only have a limited number of activities and so you will only need to create a dozen or so pictures which you can then re-use as necessary. If something unexpected comes up, you can use an exclamation mark symbol to indicate a change of plan.

Refer your child to his timetable throughout the day so that he can sense the structure and know what is about to happen. As each activity is completed remove the picture from the timetable.

Imaginative play

Once your child is copying actions and activities, try to extend his play so that he introduces some pretend elements. For example, get him to drink using an empty cup or comb his hair using a toy comb. Children start to play imaginatively either by pretending that their dolls are doing familiar activities with real objects (like sitting on the toilet) or by performing real actions but using obvious toys (making a cup of tea with a toy tea set).

Start with the simplest level of pretend play and extend it gradually by one element at a time so that you are getting a variety of actions and sequences of actions.

Gather a few toys together so you can 'pretend play' everyday activities on a doll or teddy. For instance, have a teddy and real examples of a cup, spoon, bowl, comb, blanket, rattle. Play appropriately with the articles and get your child to do the same. Move on to using toy articles instead of real ones.

Later on use other toys which reflect your child's interests – for example:

- cooking – with real or toy implements;

- eating/feeding – himself or toys;

- cars – with a toy car going shopping, to the petrol station, for a drive;

- houses – using a very large box or a sheet draped over a clothes horse or chairs;

- shops – with a basket or bag and tins or packets of food, vegetables and fruit plus a till with money;

- dressing-up box with your old clothes, shoes, hats and accessories;

- baby – with a doll and cot, nappies etc.;

- postman delivering letters on foot or in a car.

As you play sometimes pretend that one object is in fact another. You could pick up a stick and pretend it is a dog or use a box as a car.

Waldon approach

The theory

Devised by Geoffrey Waldon, this is a technique for getting children to learn the basic skills required for later cognitive development – reading, writing, mathematics, and conceptual and logical thought. It is particularly appropriate for children with autism, those who are very stubborn and those whose visual memory is better than their auditory memory.[4]

The basis of the approach is the idea that the skills of placing, sequencing, tool use, matching, sorting and pairing underlie cognitive development. Children usually experiment with these skills at a very early age; for example, you can observe young children sorting out colours or placing objects in a container and then tipping them out. They usually play happily on their own.

Children with special needs, on the other hand, often do not see the point of experimenting and exploring with objects and their different properties. The Waldon approach, therefore, seeks to give children a place and time for experimenting on their own and the opportunity for children to learn and practise these basic skills because they are so fundamental to later development.

4   The Geoffrey Waldon Centre, 636 Wilmslow Road, Didsbury, Manchester M20 0AH.

Points to remember

You are trying to create a situation in which your child is playing, exploring and experimenting on his own. You are not seeking interaction and therefore:

- Unusually, you sit behind or next to your child to do Waldon rather than in front.

- You do not speak to your child. As your child develops, he may start talking to himself while he plays. At the end of a session you could perhaps talk about all the things he has been playing with.

- Give your child a big 'well done' at the end of the session rather than praising him every time he does something. The doing of the activities should be reward enough.

This is a technique to improve cognitive skills, it is not a holistic approach. Try it for a period each day perhaps, but remember to include other activities with lots of language input and contact at other times.

How to practise Waldon

Each Waldon session should last about twenty minutes. You should always begin and end with placing because it is the easiest skill, but you can then select three or four other skills to practise each time. Work through the skills and then back again for example placing, pairing, tool use, sequencing, tool use, pairing and placing.

- Seat your child at a table and sit behind or next to him.

- Get him to complete a task using one hand and then repeat it with the other hand. Spread out the activity over the whole table so he has to reach out for objects. Try to get him to establish a rhythm in his movements.

- Start by showing your child what to do either with a hand-over-hand prompt, an elbow prompt or pointing. As he gets the idea you can reduce the aid.

- As your child progresses keep making things more difficult and complex, requiring more physical force or precision.

Waldon uses very simple household objects as well as toys, for example containers like yoghurt pots, objects to post and sort like

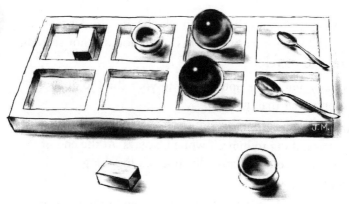

'H board' used for matching activities

bottle tops, corks and straws. Collect plastic pots, tops and containers.

To help your child place things more easily, create an 'H board' – either a wooden grid or lines drawn on a large piece of paper.

Skills

PLACING

Get your child to place objects in a container. You are aiming for him to reach out to grasp an object, using each hand alternately and to establish a regular rhythm. Use lots of objects of similar size and weight which are easy to grip. The objects can be placed on a table in front of the child or you could hold them in different places around the room so that he has to get up, collect them and then return to his seat. Also work on the need for strength so that he has to be able to post objects with some force, for example Velcro hair rollers in a small hole in the top of a tin. Use Duplo bricks, buttons, wooden blocks, bottle tops etc.

SEPARATING

Have a pile of pairs of objects (two cubes, two bottle tops, two straws, two spoons etc.). Get your child to select the pair and then put them in separate containers. Then make the differences less obvious. For example, first use a pile of buttons and bottle tops. Then encourage your child to separate by category rather than by object – you could use piles of different shells and different model animals.

PAIRING

Get your child to form pairs of objects from those in front of him. Get him to pick up one in each hand, bang them together and drop them in a container. Pair by type, colour, size etc.

MATCHING

Match objects by colour, size, texture etc. Have a tray with objects or pictures laid out and get your child to match identical ones by placing the matching one below the original on the tray.

SWITCHES OF ATTENTION

This is to enable your child to do activities which require more than one action. Start off with a two-way switch, for example a Duplo brick under each of three yoghurt pots. The child stacks the pots and places the Duplo bricks in a container. A three-way switch could be to take the lid off film cases and post the lids in one container and the cases in another. A four-way switch would be to place four cards of animals and four of colours in front of your child. Give him an envelope containing an animal and colour. He opens the envelope (1), matches the animal (2), matches the colour (3) and puts the empty envelope in a container (4). You can gradually move on to five-way switches and beyond.

TOOL USE

To begin with, get your child to practise using very simple tools, for example banging a xylophone, scooping rice or pulses into a container, pouring water, sand or rice or sweeping up buttons, stones or shells using a dustpan and brush. Then move on to more complex tools like tongs, scissors and pen control. For example, get your child to join dots, colour in a circle or copy simple shapes.

Tool use: sweeping buttons

BRICK BUILDING

Start with building simple towers then move on to more complex structures like bridges, pyramids etc., then try matching the size and weight of materials and eventually move on to copying complex designs. Use bricks, Duplo, Stickle Bricks etc.

SEQUENCING

This is concerned with the recognition of patterns. Start by creating sequences of colours – red, yellow, red, yellow – and getting your child to copy them and then continue them. Make them more complex by introducing other colours and other concepts like size and texture. For example, small, big, small, big or medium-sized, small, big, medium-sized, small, big etc. Work from left to right, then from back to front, then start changing direction. Use beads, buttons, bricks etc.

Caring Start

High/Scope is a way of working with children based on the idea that children learn best from active learning experiences which they plan and carry out themselves. It encourages children to make choices and decisions and to be responsible within their own world. High/Scope started thirty years ago in the USA and has been widely used in playgroups and schools in the UK for ten years.[5]

High/Scope aims to establish good life skills at an early age – independence, an ability to make choices, an interest in learning, and a sense of responsibility. It gives children positive attitudes to learning which stay with them throughout their lives.[6]

High/Scope has adapted its approach for parents to carry out in the home and called it Caring Start. It is not specifically for children with special needs but its ideas and approach are very applicable. High/Scope runs courses in Caring Start which are worth attending but their broad approach is outlined below.

Active learning

Children learn about their world and develop new skills by active participation in their play and not by merely observing or by

5   See Chapter 11, Resources, page 243 for contact details.
6   Schweinhart, L.J. and Weikart, D.P. (1997) *Lasting Differences: The High/Scope Pre-school Curriculum Comparison Study through Age 23*. Ypsilanti, Michigan: High/Scope Press.

being instructed. High/Scope seeks to encourage children to explore, experiment and play in order to learn by:

- giving them lots of different materials to play and experiment with;
- allowing them to handle and explore different things so that they can learn about their properties;
- giving them a choice of what they want to do and to use;
- talking to them and letting them talk as they play;
- offering support and help in solving problems and introducing new experiences but not directing them or doing it for them.

High/Scope also seeks to make children as independent as possible by giving them choices and by arranging the environment so that they are in control of their own world and not totally dependent on their parents or teachers.

If you practise Caring Start in your home, you should aim to give your child lots of different materials for play, stored in a way that is easily accessible to him and clearly labelled with pictures so that he can find the objects and return them when finished with. Children will also therefore learn that they should not touch the things in cupboards other than their own.

In your kitchen, therefore, your child could have a cupboard at his height which contains his utensils – a good range of different sizes and types of spoons, bowls, jugs etc. Then when you are cooking he can play alongside you, trying out the wooden spoon or the metal spoon, deciding on the size of bowl to use etc.

Similarly, you could have a craft cupboard with all sorts of different materials stored and labelled clearly for him to access when he wanted. He would be encouraged to play and experiment with all sorts of different objects, pencils and papers etc. to see how they worked and what their effect was. As he played you would let him experiment and explore, offering suggestions and ideas if necessary but letting him have a go and learn from his experiences.

Plan, do and review

The other centrepiece of High/Scope is the idea of getting children to think of what they are going to do and how they are going to do it. Then they execute their plan, tidy up when they have finished and finally review how it all went. This sets children up in a good routine of thinking about what they are going to do before embarking on it, then, when they have completed their activity, looking at what they have done and learning from the experience.

At home you could offer your child a choice of different activities, by showing relevant pictures or drawings of, say, a dolls' house, Duplo, painting, trainset or puzzles. He then chooses which activity or activities he wants to do and plans how he is going to do it or them. At the pre-school level, you are probably just talking about very simple plans like getting the toys off the shelf and choosing the room for the activity etc. The child then does the activity with whatever support he needs from you. If he changes his mind and does something else instead it doesn't matter but you should point out that he has changed his plans.

He would then tidy up his toys or materials, putting them away in their correct places, and then talk to you about what he has done or show you what he has done. This discussion of his achievements contributes to his self-esteem.

In some respects it is quite difficult to set up a Caring Start environment in the home, with cupboards in each room at a child's level, to allow your child the opportunity to experiment continually and to have the concentrated and uninterrupted time to carry out activities on a 'plan, do and review' basis. However, it is worth looking at the ideas to see if you can make your house work better for your child – for example, making sure his bookcase is placed at his level so he can choose a book and read it without asking you for help each time. He will thus become more used to making choices and decisions and become more independent and responsible. In the same way, when you do a specific activity at home with your child, give it a greater quality of attention. If your child decides to do painting, for example, discuss where he is going to set up his easel, what he is going to paint and with which paints and paper. Afterwards, rather than just throwing the paints back in the box, talk about what he actually did and look at the picture drawn so that you make your child think more about what he is about to do and what he has done.

CHAPTER 4

Language
Development

![THE THEORY]

What is language development?

Children learn to hear and understand what is being said to them, to copy the sounds back and then to use the words in different formations as speech. However, language is much more than speech alone. We all learn to understand body language and gesture and to pick up on the nuances of eye contact in order to communicate more effectively.[1]

Chronological development
The newborn baby

A newborn baby is unable to survive on her own so she has to communicate in some way to make sure her needs are met. A baby cries to communicate that she needs a feed, is uncomfortable or wants some companionship. Although a newborn baby does not seek eye contact, she does not avoid it. In fact, she is more interested in faces than anything else. Sometimes a baby can show that she can copy adult gestures very early, for example copying an adult by sticking out her tongue.

---

1   See Wells, G. (1985) *Language Development in the Pre-School Years.* Cambridge: Cambridge University Press. See also Law, J. (1994) *Before School: A Handbook of Approaches to Intervention with Pre-school Language Impaired Children.* AFASIC.

87

Eye contact

Eye contact

Babies soon learn to make eye contact because it is through communicating with people that they will be cared for and learn about themselves and the world about them. Making eye contact is fundamental to language development. Children have to look at people's faces to understand about communication, to pick up on the idea of taking turns to talk and to detect the emotions which people show in their eyes and facial expressions.

Smiling and vocalizing

Babies learn to smile. It is their first way of communicating apart from crying and they soon discover that it gets a good response from adults around them.

Children learn to make a greater range of sounds than just crying as they develop control over the muscles of the lips, tongue and larynx. They laugh, chuckle and squeal. They coo, blow bubbles, gurgle and trill. These noises are precursors to speech.

Turn-taking

As a child starts to vocalize she also starts to take turns with an adult. It usually starts off being barely perceptible. When holding or feeding a baby a mother will intuitively have a conversation. The baby makes a noise and the mother will copy her making a noise or silly face back, the baby then responds with gurgles, coos and attempts at copying. The child learns to 'say something', wait for a reply, then to 'say something' further and again wait for a reply. This is the basis for conversations – the idea of taking turns and of picking up on body language and facial expression to know when to talk and when to be quiet. It is a vital skill but not an obvious one that parents usually notice.

Babbling

Children continue to learn to make further sounds as they practise more with their throat and mouth, and later as they start to eat solid food and chew.

The noises children make will partly depend on the position they are placed in. A child who is lying on her back will only be able to make vowel sounds in the back of her throat (aagh) whereas a child who is sitting upright will be able to make consonant sounds at the front of her mouth (baba, dada, mama) called babbling. Babbling is the range of sounds involving consonants and vowels. Children go on to use them in long strings – for example dadadada.

Copying

Copying is fundamental to all learning and is particularly important in the development of language skills. This is because it is by copying the sounds they hear that children learn to make single words, and later to learn phrases and put together more complex sentences. Children learn to copy gestures and sounds at about the same time. They start to wave and clap in imitation of others and to copy noises if not words, especially animal noises such as moo and baa.

Understanding

Children learn to understand that a picture of a car represents a real car. When they see a picture of a car they realize it is actually a representation of the four-wheeled beast in the driveway and is not just a squiggle on a piece of paper. They then go on to understand that 'sounds', i.e. words, can symbolize or represent an actual object. When we hear the sound 'dog' it is not just a noise: we visualize a furry animal with four legs and a waggy tail.

Children pick up on the fact that sounds are words and have meanings from hearing the same words repeated again and again so that eventually they make the association. Whenever the dog appears Daddy says 'dog' and so the child associates the word with the animal. Children therefore first understand words for familiar objects and people which they hear repeatedly and which are concrete and not abstract. Children will recognize their own names and the words they hear most often like bye bye, no, mummy, daddy, siblings names etc. There is a remarkable consistency in the first words understood and said by children across families, races and cultures.

Children show they understand what is being said by responding to simple questions like 'Where's the cat?' by eye pointing, gesturing or pointing with their finger. They will also start to obey simple instructions like 'Give me the drink' or 'Come here'.

Children understand quite a wide range of words before they are able to 'say' anything.

Jargon

Children start to talk to themselves in a sing-songy way called jargon. They copy the intonation patterns of a conversation with word-like combinations and a range of sounds but it is not recognizable and has no meaning.

Pre-verbal communication

Before they learn to speak children learn to communicate by other means. They eye point by looking in the direction of something they want such as an apple, a drink or a particular toy. They then gesture with their whole hand and later point with their index finger towards what they want.

Children learn to use natural gesture to communicate: for instance, a child will wave bye bye before she learns to say it and she will learn to raise her arms up high if she wants to be lifted up or out of her cot before she can say 'up'.

First words

Often a child's first word will be a 'symbolic' noise, for example brmm brmm, moo, woof, choo choo.

First words are quite often incomprehensible to anyone but the child's own parents who will have picked up from the context that 'bibi' is used consistently to mean 'biscuit' and 'bu' means 'bus' (starting a word but not finishing it is a common feature at this stage).

First words are usually labels for people, particularly family members, animals and objects. Children then learn words for food and clothing. Often the first family name used by the child will be that of the second carer rather than the first, since he or she is probably mentioned by name more often. If the mother is the primary carer, rather than talk about herself she will probably talk about 'Daddy' as in 'Daddy's gone to work' or 'Daddy's home'.

A child may use a single 'word' to mean a whole phrase; for example, 'Daddy' could mean 'Daddy's gone', 'here's Daddy' or 'I want Daddy' and the meaning will be impossible to comprehend without the context.

First words can often be used very loosely so that all men are called 'Daddy', all vehicles 'car' and all animals 'cats'.

Two words

Children not only expand their vocabulary so that they know more words but they also start to use them in combination with others so that they can express more complex statements. 'More juice', 'Daddy gone' are common starting points. Again the exact meaning may often only be clear from the context.

Children are interested in the present (they do not develop an understanding of the past and future until later), in objects, in people – especially those close to them – in their routines, food, clothes, animals and transport. These topics will therefore be the subjects of most conversations.

Combining a noun and verb is the classic two-word combination which is the basis for further language development – man walking, dog eating, boy running. Children also combine an adjective and noun – big car, red bus.

Three words

To a two-word combination involving a noun and verb children add a further noun so they will start saying 'girl drinks milk', 'farmer drives tractor'.

Beyond three words

After children have developed the ability to use three words in combination they start developing a more grammatical structure to their language in the following way:

- They ask what and who questions and use pronouns such as I, me and you.
- They start using more pronouns (e.g. him and her), plurals (horses, glasses) and prepositions (in, on, under). They carry out simple conversations and can talk about the past and present. They start asking where questions.
- They ask why, when and how questions.

By the time they start school children's speech is usually grammatically and phonetically correct.

Parallel development

Uses of language

Children initially use language to make comments on what they can see: 'Look car' and to ask for things they need and want: 'Biscuit'. Gradually they use language not only in longer forms (more words) but with more complexity and flexibility to ask questions – 'Where's Daddy?' – to request information – 'Why is it raining?' – to request attention – 'How do you do this?' – and to negotiate with others – 'You pull this string and I'll pull that one'.

Pronunciation

Children develop the ability over time to make different sounds, to distinguish between all the different sounds they hear and to be able to pronounce all consonants correctly. At school age children may still be confusing some sounds, such as s, f, and th.

Attention spans

In parallel with the development of language, children learn to extend their attention spans. When they are very young, children are initially very easily distracted from what they are doing. If they are playing with a train but see an interesting car they will immediately transfer their attention.

They later become fixated on one activity, learn to cut out all distractions and will not tolerate any intervention because they cannot cope with doing two things at once.

Gradually they become able to cope with doing an activity and having someone give information and advice at the same time. They are able to do their task and at the same time listen to simple and relevant instructions. Later they can switch their attention between their activity and more complex instructions (see note on page 55).

GAMES AND ACTIVITIES

General guidelines

The following are some pointers for ways to make it easier for your child to understand you.

- Speak simply and clearly. Don't wrap up important words in lots of flowery language but use the important words on their own. Make it easy for your child to get the message. Don't say 'I would rather you didn't bang that knife on the table', say 'No banging'. Don't say 'Why don't you put the brick in the bucket?' say 'Brick in'.

- Make your language fit your child's level of understanding and just be one step beyond. So if she uses one word, use two and encourage her to use two back. Adapt your language as your child progresses.

- Repeat simple phrases and words over and over again at every opportunity.

- Babies and children respond to a high-pitched voice which is why adults use it naturally. Don't stop using this voice even though your child is no longer a small baby.

- Talk to your child with an interesting, sing-songy voice. Vary your tone to maintain your child's attention. A flat, monotonous tone is very dull.

- Make sure your facial expressions and tone of voice give the same message as your language. Communication is more complex than just understanding the spoken word. We all listen to tone and interpret body language as well as the words themselves in order to understand the full message we are being given. Children are no different and if they are finding communication a problem it does not help them if you are saying 'no' very forcefully with a big grin on your face. (Later children will learn to deal with mixed messages.)

- Use natural gesture when you speak as it will aid understanding.

- Respond immediately to any communication your child makes with you whether it be a smile, a gesture or a word. Make her understand that communication works.

- Don't overcorrect your child because it will tend to make her shy of attempting new words and language. Just say 'yes' and repeat back what your child was trying to say. For example, if your child says 'bibi' for biscuit say 'Yes, biscuit'.

- Sing to your child. Children and adults have an innate musicality and it is worth taking advantage of it. Some children who do not respond to the spoken word will respond much better when they have instructions or information sung to them.

- Speech therapists say that 'please' and 'thank you' are not useful words in terms of communication and should only be introduced once a child has a fairly extensive vocabulary. There is nothing more unhelpful than a situation where a child is asked what she wants and she just says 'please'. She should first be taught drink, toilet, food, biscuit and so on.

- If your child has a hearing impairment but no other delay, consult a speech therapist or adviser for the hearing impaired for the best approach to communication development.

Chronological development
Eye contact

If your child does not make eye contact readily then work on it. Even if she already has more advanced skills, it is important that she makes good eye contact in order to learn language.

You must always try to be directly in front of and close to your child so that she cannot avoid your gaze. If necessary get down to her level. Remember you are much bigger than her. Crouch down or lie down on the floor. Move yourself, not your child. Never physically force her to look at you even though you may have to work very hard to get her to look at you.

Always aim to get eye contact before starting any new game or activity. Once you have got eye contact, reward it immediately with the new toy or game.

Make your face 'interesting' for your child so that she wants to look at you. If she just sees a blank and bored expression she won't be tempted, but she might be if you make an over the top effort. You could:

- give lots of big smiles;
- make silly faces – waggle your eyebrows, screw up your face;
- make silly noises;
- wear unusual hats, glasses (large, colourful or silly), sunglasses, dangly earrings or a red nose;
- wear masks;
- use face paints.

Sometimes you can attract a child's attention by blowing softly on her cheek or by being very still and silent. A change may gain more attention than lots of frenetic activity.

Take an object that has caught your child's attention and bring it to your face. Her eyes will usually follow it. Reward the eye contact by playing with the toy and then build on your success by doing it again with the same or a different toy.

Alternatively, you can hide a toy behind your head, wait for eye contact and then show the toy. Use a favourite toy, the spoon at meal times or a squeaky toy where you have the added interest of a noise.

Play peek-a-boo games using:

- scarves (ordinary or chiffon/semi-transparent);
- teatowels in the kitchen;
- towels in the bathroom;
- sheets when changing bedlinen;
- washing on the line;
- curtains;
- furniture and doors;
- clothes when getting dressed and undressed;
- bibs when pulling them on and off;
- your hands on your child's face and on your own;
- your child's hands on her face and your own.

When playing peek-a-boo sing the following using a scarf to hide your child:

I can play peek-a-boo
Are you there? Yes I am
Are you there? Yes I am
Peek-a peek-a peek-a peek-a booooo.

Sing songs with your child sitting on your knee and looking directly at you. For instance:

Row, row, row your boat gently down the stream
Merrily, merrily, merrily, merrily life is but a dream.

See-saw Margery Daw
Johnny shall have a new master
He shall have but a penny a day
Because he can't work any faster.

Horsey, horsey don't you stop
Just let your feet go clippety clop
Your tail goes swish and your wheels go round
Giddy up we're homeward bound.

This is the way the ladies ride
Trot trot trot
This is the way the farmer rides
Hobble dee hoy, Hobble dee hoy
This is the way the plough boys ride
A-gallop a-gallop and into the ditch.
(*Or one of the hundreds of different versions.*)
Bounce your child up and down and 'drop' her when you go 'into the ditch'.

Bumpty bumpty bumpty bump
As if I was riding my charger
Bumpty bumpty bumpty bump
As proud as an Indian Rajah
All the girls declare
That I'm a gay old stager
Hey, hey clear the way
Here comes the galloping major.

Have you ever ever ever in your long legged life
Seen a long legged sailor with a long legged wife
No I've never never never in my long legged life
Seen a long legged sailor with a long legged wife.
Lay your child flat on her back and hold her legs by the ankles moving them
backwards and forwards, with knees bent, rather like a cycling motion.

Join a child who is engaging in solitary play by mirroring her actions with the same or similar toys. Use some language but do not be afraid of silence.

Waiting

As a forerunner to turn-taking games try to extend your child's concentration so she is made to wait, even if it is for seconds, rather than have an instant response. For example:

- Play games where a ball or car goes down a tube and reappears a few moments later.

- Blow bubbles so that your child has to wait a few moments for the next one to appear.

Turn-taking

Remember that children with special needs can take a long time to respond so always give your child longer to reply than you feel is natural. When you think she is not going to take her turn remember to count to ten again to give her extra time.

- Sit your child on your knee or opposite you and watch for any sounds or faces your child makes and then respond similarly. Give an exaggerated response and then wait for her to take her turn. Meal times or quiet times are also good

Taking turns to put oranges in a bowl

for picking up on any communication attempts your child might make.

- Roll a ball or push a car to your child and get her to return it to you. If you do it sitting opposite each other at a table, it is good for eye contact too.

- You can turn many games into turn-taking games, for example putting things into a container, posting shapes, drawing or completing a puzzle. Choose something that your child enjoys.

- Take turns when feeding animals, either a pet or on a children's farm.

Understanding that language means something

Children have to learn that the noise they hear has a meaning. The following games help a child to learn that words indicate that something interesting is going to happen!

Anticipation rhymes and songs

Use the appropriate actions to go with the following rhymes and songs.

IN THE SWIMMING POOL

The swimming pool is a good place for doing rhymes like:

- 'Humpty Dumpty' (sit your child on the side of the swimming pool and get him to jump in at the right moment);

- 'Ring a ring o' roses' (hold your child in your arms and fall down then jump up);

- 'The wheels on the bus' (making movements in the water, blowing bubbles for the bell, bounce your child up and down etc.);

- 'Down in the water, down in the sea, playing with the fishes, one two three'.

You can also do lots of jumping 'in', getting 'out', jumping 'up' and 'down'.

Round and round the garden like a teddy bear
One step, two steps and tickle you under there.

This little piggy went to market, this little piggy stayed at home
This little piggy had roast beef and this little piggy had none
And this little piggy cried wee wee wee all the way home.

KNEE RIDES

Humpty Dumpty sat on the wall, Humpty Dumpty had a great fall
All the king's horses and all the king's men couldn't put Humpty
together again.

Walk walk walk trot trot trot canter canter canter and over the fence.
Bounce your child up high when you go 'over the fence'.

This is the way the ladies ride…
For the words see p.96 above.

Ring a ring o' roses
A pocketful of posies
A-tishoo, a-tishoo
We all fall down.

> Fishes in the water
> Fishes in the sea
> We all jump up
> With a one two three.

The grand old duke of York, he had ten thousand men
He marched them up to the top of the hill and he marched them
down again.
And when they were up they were up
And when they were down they were down
And when they were only half way up they were neither up nor
down.

Ready, steady, go

Play 'Ready, steady, go' games because they will teach your child
that 'go' means something is going to happen. For example, say
'Ready, steady, go' and then roll a ball, push a car, push your child
fast in her pushchair or knock a brick tower down. Just make
something exciting happen. Increase the pause between 'steady'
and 'go' to maximize anticipation and increase concentration.
Then you can encourage your child to perform the action instead

of you, so you say 'ready, steady, go' and she knocks down the bricks or throws the ball.

Sing to your child

Find a tune that you like, for example 'Here we go round the mulberry bush' or 'The farmer's in his den' and make up your own words to suit the occasion. 'This is the way we do the puzzle', 'This is the way we eat our yoghurt', 'Nick is on the bed', 'Christopher's doing a poo'. It becomes very easy and it is also a good way of easing tension. Children love 'live music' and cannot distinguish between you and Pavarotti. So sing as badly as you like and do not feel embarrassed.

> If Harriet wants more of something and cannot have it, she gets very upset but singing 'no more' instead of saying it calms her and me down and usually makes us all smile.

Use exaggerated language like 'Noooooo' instead of 'No' to make language more interesting and more understandable.

Copying

Children learn to copy you by first seeing you copy them.

To encourage your child to copy the sounds you make first, copy the sounds she makes. She will then learn to copy you back. When your child makes noises such as coos or gurgles, copy them back to her.

At other times make the sounds you have heard your child making, whatever they are, and see if she will copy you back. Pushchair walks, car journeys and bath times are good times because children are more able to concentrate and less likely to be distracted.

Use natural gestures frequently and see if your child will copy them. For example, wave goodbye, say 'shhh' with your finger to your lips, put a hand up to your ear for 'listen', or put your fingers to your nose for 'pooey nappy'.

See also Chapter 3, pages 58–60, for other games to encourage copying skills.

Encouraging sounds

Children vary as to when they are most vocal. Some children are most vocal after or during a meal when muscles have been exercised, some like the bath where noises are exaggerated, and others are most vocal in the car or pushchair when they are not distracted by other things. Follow their lead. Children need to develop the muscles of the mouth and throat to make a full range of sounds. So, although some of these ideas may not appear to be related to making sounds, they are nevertheless important for strengthening different muscles.

- Tickling and laughing games – a chuckle and laugh is a baby's next way of communicating after crying and smiling.

- Make funny noises and faces to your child and encourage your child to copy. If she responds reward her exaggeratedly.

- While both of you are looking at yourselves in a mirror, try to get your child to copy your facial expressions and noises.

- Play games involving blowing. Blow through straws into water, play blow football or move pieces of tissue paper by blowing through a straw. Blow musical instruments like mouth organs, whistles, party whistles, kazoos, pipes, recorders and trumpets. See what happens if you blow flimsy scarves, feathers, bubbles, light mobiles, pieces of ripped-up paper and tissues. Blow out birthday cake candles. Blow bubbles under the water in the bath or swimming pool. Blow dandelion clocks in the summer.

Blowing bubbles

- Get your child to suck on straws for drinking or use straws to pick up paper fish, Smarties, peas etc.

- Get her to lick things like stickers, stamps and envelopes. Encourage her to lick food from around her mouth. Get her to lick ice-creams and lollies.

- Eating chewy and lumpy food gets all the jaw muscles working and increases the range of sounds a child can make so you should encourage your child to move from pureed food to lumpy food. If your child has a problem eating lumpy or chewy food then you should consult your speech therapist.

- As you play and read books make lots of symbolic sounds – brmm brmm, moo, woof, miaow, baa, tick tock, clip clop etc. – because these are often the first meaningful sounds a child will make.

- Play games your child enjoys, then stop and wait for her to show that she wants more by vocalizing. Say 'more' or 'again' and repeat the game. Find a game that is really motivating for your child. It might be tickling, singing or rough and tumble games.

- Sing rhymes such as the following:

  > Row row row your boat gently down the stream
  > If you see a crocodile don't forget to scream. Aaaaaagh! *(get your child to say Aaaagh)*

  > Hey diddle diddle, the cat and the fiddle
  > The cow jumped over the moon
  > The little dog laughed
  > Ha! *(get your child to laugh before continuing)*
  > To see such fun
  > And the dish ran away with the spoon.

- Try humming songs like lullabies.

Natasha had a protruding tongue from birth and for three years only vocalized 'ee' with her mouth wide open and tongue sticking out. We tried everything to bring her lips together such as massaging her mouth, putting a finger under her chin to encourage the swallowing reflex, telling her to close her mouth and experimenting will all sorts of food on her lips. One day I lay on a bean bag and put Natasha on my tummy. There was some gentle piped music on the cassette in the background. I started to hum and all of a sudden Natasha started humming too. Six months later she can say baa baa and mama.

- You can buy or borrow mobiles which move or toys which vibrate when a sound is made. They give children a wonderful incentive to make sounds.

Early communication skills

Try to think of language as communication rather than just speaking. Everyone hopes speech will come but it may take time so you and your child need to find other ways to communicate. This will enable your child to develop all her skills and relieve some of the frustration you will both feel if your child cannot express her needs and desires. In addition, improving pre-language skills will increase the chances that language will develop. If her speech is delayed, be sensitive to the other ways in which your child is actually communicating and encourage her. If she sees the advantages of communicating she is much more likely to want to learn to speak.

- All attempts and efforts to communicate should be rewarded with lots of praise and encouragement to begin with. If you think your child might be trying to communicate by some means, perhaps eye-pointing (i.e. looks specifically at something, see p.90) or vocalizing, give her the benefit of the doubt.

- Respond immediately to what your child is communicating to show that you are interested and understand her. If she eye-points at a book offer him the book. If she vocalizes at the sight of the cat say 'Yes, it's the cat'. If she is asking for something, you don't have to say 'yes' all the time but you should acknowledge that she is trying to communicate and not ignore her, otherwise she might not be so keen to 'talk'.

Emma's third sign was biscuit and we were delighted. Obviously we rewarded her with a biscuit each time so that she saw the benefits of communicating. However after five biscuits (even broken into hundreds of fragments) we did have to start saying 'no'!

- Always reinforce what your child is trying to tell you by saying it back. For example if your child eye-points at a drink or brings a cup to you respond by saying 'Jane wants a drink? Here's the drink'.

- Don't anticipate your child's every need. Give her the opportunity to make a request, show she is hungry or demand a change. If you anticipate her all the time there will be no need for communication.

- The following are ways in which children communicate before they have speech.

Crying

A baby expresses her unhappiness by crying and parents learn to understand what their child's needs are by the nature of her cry. It might be food, a nappy change, wind, sleep or cuddles. Children with a communication problem may use this method for some time, as it is effective.

Early communication skills

Laughing

By laughing children are also communicating that they are having fun and enjoying themselves. Parents naturally want to repeat actions which get a good response from their child.

Signs of anticipation

An early form of communication is showing signs of anticipation. For example, children start wriggling when they hear the first words of tickling songs and knee rides because they know something fun is going to happen.

Eye-pointing

Children use eye-pointing to express their needs or respond to questions but parents have to be quite sensitive to pick it up. If you ask your child to show you the picture of the dog, she may not point with her finger but may look at the dog instead. This shows that she understands you and is responding to you. Similarly, your child may eye-point to things around the house that she wants. If your child is sitting on your knee looking at a book, it is difficult to pick up on eye-pointing, so it may be worth sitting opposite her.

Pointing

Children point with their finger or gesture with their whole hand to indicate their needs or respond to a request. They also point generally as a way of getting you to tell them about the world and interact with them. To encourage pointing as a way of comm-unicating try the following:

- Hold a toy or food slightly out of reach and encourage your child to reach for it or point to it to show she wants it.

- Sing 'Wind the bobbin up' with appropriate gestures (see Chapter 3, p.59, for the words).

- Play teasing games where you offer your child a toy and then pull it away as she reaches for it.

- Try holding your child's hand in yours and pointing at pictures in books.

- Have pictures of things your child likes, for example food at meal-times or toys when you are playing, and ask her to point to what she wants.

Liam's main difficulty has been the acquisition and use of language, but we have found that he can ask for what he wants using pictures. I photographed a great number of familiar household objects, toys and things he particularly liked, had them laminated and velcroed them to a board which we hang on the kitchen door. Now he can bring the picture as his way of asking for something. The only problem we had with this was that for a while every time he walked past the board he would select the biscuit picture! We now leave that one off the board if he asks too much. This has been a big help to Liam and us.

For other ideas see Chapter 5, pages 145–146.

The direct approach

If children cannot communicate verbally they often bring you the actual object to tell you what they want. If your child brings a book it probably means 'read to me', an empty cup means 'I'm thirsty.'

Children take adults by the hand and lead them to what they want. Sometimes they may take your hand and place it on the relevant object. It is a very effective way of communicating if your child has not got the language to say 'Please could you get the puzzle out of the cupboard for me'.

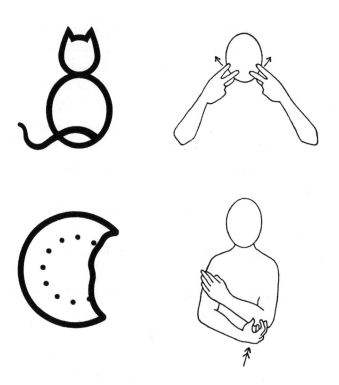

Makaton sign and symbol for biscuit and cat

Gestures

Children use natural gesture to communicate. For example, they might show that they want to be lifted up by raising their hands. Use natural gesture to accompany your normal speech.

Signing systems

A natural extension of gesture is to introduce signs. Young children with communication problems are often introduced to Makaton or Signalong which are signing systems in which the spoken word is accompanied by a sign. The signs are derived from British Sign Language and some have been modified to be expressive and clear with large arm movements rather than small fiddly ones. Children therefore learn language in a multi-sensory way. They hear the word spoken and they see a sign which provides a visual reinforcement. They can communicate back either with the word if they can say it, or with the sign, or both. Many parents fear that if their child learns to sign she will never speak but this is certainly not the case. All the evidence suggests that signs aid speech. Although it is impossible to prove the success or otherwise of such systems, research has shown that children use the signs while they need to and when they can say the words they automatically drop the signs. Some children use Makaton for a very short period and then start speaking; some use it for a long time and find it really helpful; while for others it does not seem to make a difference.

Both Makaton and Signalong only sign the most important words in a sentence, not each and every word. For example if you asked 'Do you want a drink?' you could just sign 'drink'.

We found Makaton to be a life-saver. Christopher first learnt to sign 'drink' and 'bird' at about two years old. He learnt 'biscuit' and 'more' at about two and a half and from about three his vocabulary exploded. He doesn't need Makaton so much to understand what people are saying but it is his only way to express himself. At four, however, he has just begun to vocalize. Before he could sign he showed considerable frustration, anger and unhappiness but they have been relieved to an extent by signing. His younger brother Nicholas started signing when he was one and I must admit I panicked momentarily but as he learns to say the words he drops the signs and his combination of words and signs makes him extremely communicative.

Makaton and Signalong have a somewhat different approach to each other but they share the same basic idea. Makaton is more widely used but it tends to depend on where you live and it is worth finding out which system is used in your area so that you work in harmony with your child's speech therapist and school. See Chapter 11, pages 244 and 251, for more details of both organizations.

How to use signs with your child

Makaton and Signalong run courses on their signing systems which are vital if you plan to use signs but if you want to start straightaway, ask someone to show you some signs.

- Select three or four words which are most relevant to your child. Choose words which your child will be motivated to understand and use back, for example: drink, biscuit, more and dog. There is not much point teaching her cigarette, boss or work. Learn the signs and don't feel self-conscious about using them everywhere and anywhere.

- Whenever you use the chosen words in your conversation give the sign too. Get everyone who cares for your child to do the same – friends, grandparents, playgroups.

- Always say the words when you use the signs, they are not a replacement for speech.

- Make sure your child is looking at you when you sign otherwise you will be wasting your time.

As your child shows that she understands or can use the signs, keep one step ahead by introducing three or four more, again choosing signs which are most relevant to her.

Understanding the meaning of words

When children do not speak, parents often focus on getting them to talk by asking them to name things and copy sounds. It is more important for parents to focus on increasing their child's understanding of language since understanding is the key to speech.

- In daily life, reduce your language to very simple words as described in General Guidelines, page 93 above. Do not be tempted to fill in silences with waffle. Repeat everything over and over again. It may be very tedious for you but your child needs to hear a word repeatedly before she makes the connection between the word and the object, place or concept.

- Talk about the 'here and now'. Children do not develop a sense of past and future for some time. Talk about objects and activities which have meaning for your child, not about abstract notions or space travel.

- Remember children get fed up with naming things which they know adults really know. If you are labelling things, try to do so in context. Alternatively, make a game by putting objects in a bag and get your child to choose one without your seeing and tell you what it is.

- If your child expresses her needs non-verbally, by signing or pointing, always state what she has communicated in very simple language. 'You want a drink', 'That's milk', 'You want the video'.

- Give a running commentary on what you are doing with your child as you play and as you do everyday things like changing nappies and washing. Use very simple (but normal) language to aid her understanding.

- Create an album with clear photographs of your child's own toys and familiar objects like her teddy bear, favourite beaker, car, highchair, bath, pet, family and so on. Look through the album with your child naming the pictures. Try to have just two pictures on each page. Ask your child to point to a specific picture given a choice of two or three.

- Create a scrapbook with images your child likes cut from magazines, newspapers and catalogues. If she likes particular types of objects like animals or vehicles choose those. Bought picture books can often be full of pictures which are of no interest to your child.

- Look at very simple picture books with your child. Initially pictures must be very clear and easily understood. Photographs are especially good (for example the 'What's That' series by Campbell Books). Point to and name each picture and ask your child to find a named picture given a choice of two or three. (If there are too many on a page cover some up.) Always start by asking her to select her favourite picture which you know she will select, then build on your success.

- Use everyday events to expand knowledge. For instance, you could take the theme 'getting dressed':

- as you are dressing your child name the different items of clothing

- together make a book of clothing pictures taken from magazines and catalogues

- dress a teddy or doll

- give opportunities to choose between two items. For example, 'which shirt do you want to wear?'

- ask 'where is…?' questions

- pretend to forget an article or ask 'What do we need?'

- Ask very simple questions like 'Where's the ball?', 'Where's Mummy?', or make simple requests 'Give me the spoon', 'Give me teddy'. If she does not respond, you respond for her saying 'Here's the ball', 'There's Mummy', and 'I've got the spoon'.

- Be silly. Put socks on your ears and get your child to tell you where they go. Put your socks on her feet and try to get hers on yours!

- Body parts are some of the first words children learn and there are lots of games you can play. You could sing 'Round and round the garden', 'This little piggy went to market', 'Head, shoulders, knees and toes'. Play tickling games, naming the bits you are tickling. Name body parts in the bath – the most natural time. See Chapter 8, pages 189–190, for other ideas.

First words

There is nothing you can do to make a child say her first words. They will come if the child has the understanding, the ability to vocalize or sign and the opportunity. Concentrate on all the games listed in the sections Understanding the meaning of words and Encouraging sounds. It is by talking to your child and playing with her, that you are most likely to help her language development. It also helps to introduce a few key signs from Makaton or Signalong.

Expanding into two-word phrases

A child has to understand two-word phrases before she will be able to use them. Once a child has a reasonable level of vocabulary, it is good to start combining words. Nouns are good for labelling things but speech therapists say that they are not actually very useful in terms of communication. Being able to say that something is a tree or a house won't get you very far. You really want to say something like 'red house', 'I want the house' or 'go into the house'. So it is important to concentrate on verbs (walk, run, sleep, eat, go, give) and prepositions (in, on, under). Adjectives come later (red, big, hot etc.).

It is important to know what 'understanding two words' means. It means understanding two 'information carrying' words. Therefore words like 'the' and 'a' don't count. In addition, a child has to demonstrate that she is understanding the words, not just picking up what is meant by the context. If you give a child a doll and a cup and tell her that the doll wants a drink and she gives the doll a drink, it does not demonstrate much because there is little else she could do. If however there is a comb, a drink, a doll and a teddy and she gives the doll a drink on request it would demonstrate two-word understanding.

- When your child is consistently saying single words, respond with a second. For instance, if she says 'dog', respond by saying 'dog eating' or 'dog sleeping'. If she asks for 'more' ask her to say 'more carrot' or 'more milk'.

- To practise verbs comment on things you see around you, for instance dog running, bird flying, baby crying, cat sleeping and car stopping.

- Use two word commands where your child has to show that she understands two words used together. 'Kiss granny' (when someone else is present as well) or 'Kick the ball' (where there are other objects around).

- Look at books and talk about what people, animals and things are doing.

- Use pictures of people doing things, for instance a man drinking, a woman driving and a child crying and ask your child to select the correct picture and to say what is happening,

- In everyday situations around the house expand your language into two-word phrases. Instead of just saying 'eating', 'drinking' or 'washing', say 'eating the bread', 'drinking the milk', 'washing my hands', 'brushing my hair'.

- Use dolls or teddies and everyday objects to mime activities which you can then talk about in two-word phrases. 'Dolly is eating', 'Teddy is sleeping', 'Dolly is reading'.

Learning abstract concepts

Children need lots of opportunities for generalizing abstract concepts, otherwise it is difficult for them to pick up their true meaning.

- Use every opportunity in your daily life to talk about abstract concepts like hot/cold, up/down, out/in, open/closed, high/low and heavy/light.

- Look at children's books which illustrate these concepts in different ways.

Expanding into three-word phrases

Children must demonstrate that they are understanding and using three different 'information-carrying' words, not just picking up on context.

- When your child is consistently giving two-word phrases respond with a third word. For example 'Daddy gone' becomes 'Daddy's gone to work', 'Daddy's gone in the car' or 'Daddy's gone out'.

- Talk about the objects or activities your child is interested in. If she likes trains, talk about the railway set and what is going on – trains, carriages, trucks, stations, drivers, passengers, going, stopping, pulling, up, down, through, bridges, tunnels etc.

- Do things with your child which will generate lots of talking. If you are shopping, talk about what you are buying – its name, its colour, its size and what you will do with it. If you are gardening talk about digging, plants, flowers, colours, animals and birds.

- Read books together, talk about the pictures and the story.

- Play together: this is the main way children pick up language.

- Talk about everyday routines.

- At bed-time or bath-time or when Daddy or Mummy comes home, talk about things you have done during the day.

Beyond three words

If your child is using three words together she will probably continue to develop her language so that it gradually becomes more grammatically correct. Further language development becomes more and more specific and is therefore beyond the scope of this book. However, you can still encourage the use of more complex sentences by using the ideas listed above.

Parallel development

Carolyn Smith's approach

Dr Carolyn Smith is an educational psychologist on the Isle of Wight who has conducted research into early communication, based on the work of J Bruner,[2] and has devised the following approach which will be the basis of a forthcoming books.[3] It emphasizes the need to return to the foundations of speech and communication, eye contact and turn-taking, because only once these are established fully will communication proceed.

Play ideas

Watch your child at play and observe what she can do and likes doing on her own. It may be shaking a rattle, putting bricks in a container, drawing, playing with a doll or running a train along a track. It does not matter how simple it is because it is going to be the vehicle for language development.

Once you have decided what activity your child likes, take two identical or similar sets of toys so that you can mirror her. For instance, take two buckets with bricks and sit opposite and close to your child. Give one bucket to her and use one yourself. Copy exactly what she is doing. Mirror her but do not instruct her. You are trying to get her interest and thereby her co-operation.

Your child will be intrigued and look at you to watch you copying her actions; thereby making eye contact. Repeat this as much as you can to extend eye contact.

---

2   See Bruner, J. (1983) *Child Talk*. Oxford: Oxford University Press; Bruner, J. (1990) Acts of Meaning. Cambridge, Massachusetts: Harvard University Press; and Nadel, J. and Camaioni, L. (eds) (1993) *New Perspectives in Early Communication Development*. London: Routledge.

3   Smith, C. and Fluck, M. (forthcoming) *Constructing Interpersonal Pre-linguistic Processes to Promote Language Development in Young Children with Deviant or Delayed Communication Skills*; and Smith, C. (unpublished) *PRELIM: Pre-linguistic Intervention Methods: A Workshop Manual for a Scheme to Promote Pre-linguistic Communication Processes*.

Mirror what your child is doing

You can start talking about what you are doing. Keep all language to a minimum to aid understanding, for example 'brick in', 'brick out' or 'brick on'.

This will lead to turn-taking. Your child will put a brick in the bucket then look at you and wait for you to copy her by putting a brick in the bucket. You do this and then look at her and wait while she puts another brick in the bucket. You are taking turns – having a conversation.

Your child is learning that she can get you to copy her – she is learning to control you which is a vital skill.

After you have been copying your child's actions you can start extending the game by doing something different and seeing if your child will copy you. As your child's understanding increases you can start using more complex language in your play.

Once her play with an adult is well established you can introduce another child in a structured setting, continuing the same ideas so that your child can learn to talk to and play appropriately with her peers.

Music therapy

Music therapy aims to enable children and adults to use music as a means of communication and self-expression. Young children with special needs who have problems communicating, interacting and expressing themselves through language may be stimulated to respond by listening to and making music. Music therapists use music to arouse and engage the child and then to develop a relationship with her.

At a very simple level, set aside some time during the day to play with music. Try singing songs, clapping your hands to rhythms and encouraging your child to play with instruments like tambourines, drums and chime bars. Encourage your child to listen to the sounds you make. Try copying what she plays on the instruments in order to develop an idea of turn-taking. Also encourage her to vocalize or play an instrument to accompany songs and music.[4]

Making music with your child in this way will encourage listening skills, turn-taking and vocalization which help language skills.

Alternatively, or in addition, contact the British Society for Music Therapy (see Chapter 11, p.238), for names of music therapists in your area.

---

4   See Streeter, E. (1993) *Making Music with the Young Child with Special Needs.* London: Jessica Kingsley Publishers.

CHAPTER 5

Physical Development

What is physical development?

Included in this section are all aspects of controlling the body, its muscles and its movements. The chapter has been subdivided into 'Development of gross motor skills', which includes all larger movements of legs and arm, and 'Development of fine motor skills', which includes the delicate movements of the hands and fingers.

GROSS MOTOR SKILLS
Chronological development
The newborn baby

When babies are born they are totally dependent on their parents for help to survive but they do have the following reflexes, some of which are vital for their survival while others are throwbacks to our past evolution:

- sucking and swallowing;
- rooting for the mother's nipple;
- grasping;
- walking (if a newborn baby is supported in standing position on a firm surface he will make steps);
- startle or Moro (if a baby thinks he is going to be dropped he throws his arms back with open hands and then slowly brings his arms back together with clenched fists).

Newborn babies have very little muscle control and have to be supported and held securely. However in the first months and years of life, the brain develops its ability to control the muscles and thereby the movements of the body. With the exception of those with very tight tendons who may have problems with sitting and find it easier to stand than sit, children gain control over their bodies in the same order because their physical development is governed by two fundamental laws.

1. Development proceeds from top to bottom (cephalocaudal law) – children learn to control their necks, then their backs, their hips and finally their legs. This is reflected in heads growing first and looking out of proportion to bodies.

2. Development proceeds from the inside to the outside (proximodistal law). This is reflected in hands and feet seeming small compared to the rest of a baby's body. Also children learn to support themselves on their elbows before their hands and they kneel before they can stand.

Physical development comes from active play. A child kicking his legs is developing his muscles. Similarly every time a child attempts to lift his head he is strengthening his muscles and developing his ability to control his movements.

Head control

Newborn babies are not able to support their heads. They gradually develop their neck muscles so that they can support their heads and look around while their backs are supported in a sitting position or while being drawn up by their arms from the lying to the sitting position. As the neck muscles and those at the top of the spine strengthen, babies become able to lift their heads up while lying on their tummies.

Forearm and extended arm support

While lying on their tummies, they learn to raise their chests off the ground first by supporting themselves on their forearms with arms bent and then on their hands with their arms extended straight in front of them.

Rolling over

Babies first roll from their sides to their backs and later from their backs to their tummies.

Weight-bearing on forearms and extended arms

Sitting up

When newborn babies are placed in a sitting position they collapse forward in a rounded heap with a curved back. As their back muscles strengthen they need less and less support either from adults supporting them or from cushions at the base of the spine. Eventually they can sit unaided without risk of falling over backwards or sideways. When they lose balance they know how to save themselves by propping (putting their hand down to the floor by their side).

Then they learn to turn sideways to pick up toys as well as lean forwards and backwards without toppling over.

Crawling

Children strengthen their hips and legs through vigorous kicking, either of alternate legs or of both legs together. They then learn to move around using one of a variety of methods. Some children crawl in the conventional way on hands and knees, some bear crawl on hands and feet; some do commando crawling on their tummies; while others use bottom shuffling instead and never crawl.

Some parents feel that crawling is a rather pointless stage on the way to walking and try to hurry children to stand up and walk. However, crawling is in fact an important skill because it makes children bear weight through their arms, thus

Crawling

strengthening the shoulders, arms and hands. It is this which gives children the strength and control to be able to develop fine motor skills like drawing and writing later on.

High kneeling

Children learn to kneel with their bodies straight to their knees, thus bearing weight through their hips. This is a step towards learning to stand up because the muscles around the hips only develop through taking weight.

High stride kneeling

While in the high kneeling position, children learn to place one foot flat on the ground, take their weight over this foot and then push themselves into a standing position.

Standing

In order to stand up children need to be able to stretch out their hips and knees and have the muscle power and balance to bear weight. Children first stand while holding onto furniture or people for balance and support before they are able to stand on their own.

Walking

Before walking independently children must be able to stand and bounce up and down flexing their knees. They learn to cruise, i.e. walk sideways around furniture before walking forwards, holding an adult's hands or pushing a trolley or piece of furniture. Gradually as strength and confidence increase they need less support until finally they can walk alone for a few steps.

Initially, children walk with their legs far apart and their arms high for balance. They are very unsteady tripping and stumbling frequently and find it difficult to stop, change direction or look down.

As children become more agile, their feet come closer together and point forwards rather than outwards and they have a more regular stride pattern. They are able to change direction, bend down to pick up things from the floor and carry objects as they walk. They learn to push and pull toys and to walk backwards.

Climbing up and down stairs

Once they can crawl children soon start to climb up furniture and steps. They climb in the crawling position using their knees and hands. They then climb using their feet rather than their knees which they place on alternate steps. Eventually they stand up straight in an adult posture but need to hold on to a handrail or someone's hand for support. Initially they put both feet on each step before finally learning to put alternate feet on alternate steps.

Coming down stairs is more difficult than going up. Initially children either slide down on their tummies feet first or bump down on their bottoms. Eventually they take an upright posture and walk down, first holding the rail and placing two feet on each step and then putting alternate feet on alternate steps.

Balance

An improvement in balance underlies much of children's later physical development. Children learn to stand on one leg, hop, walk on a narrow beam or line and negotiate stepping stones.

Running

The transition from walking to running happens quite gradually. Children speed up their walking over time until they are able to run. They are liable to trip and fall initially but they learn to move around skilfully, turn sharp corners, carry, pull or push objects as they go, speed up and slow down.

Catching, throwing and kicking a ball

Children learn to catch large balls when thrown gently into their arms by putting their arms out rigidly. They gradually learn to bend their arms and to catch smaller balls and from a greater distance.

Children learn to let a ball drop from their arms before being able to throw it. They improve their skills in terms of both the direction and strength of their aim.

Kicking begins with children walking into a ball and kicking it accidentally; then they learn to kick standing still and later on the run, balancing on one leg. First kicks are very gentle but gradually children gain strength and control.

Jumping

Children start trying to jump by bending their knees but their feet do not actually leave the ground. They first jump on the spot and then learn to jump off objects such as low steps and logs before being able to do a series of jumps without falling over.

FINE MOTOR SKILLS
Chronological development
The newborn baby

Newborn babies keep their hands closed tightly in the reflex grip.

Grasp and release

After the first few weeks they lose this reflex and have to practise until they have achieved the control to grasp objects again. Gripping something is a complex action requiring children to be able to control their arm and hand movements, turn their heads to see the object and focus their eyes on it.

Babies bring their hands in front of their eyes and examine them. They are learning the rudiments of hand–eye co-ordination. They play with their hands working out what they can do and how to get them to the right place. Initially they bat at objects dangled in front of them such as rattles strung across a pram or a baby gym.

They then learn to grasp an object with their whole hand, then to pass it from hand to hand and then to bang two objects together. Children initially grasp objects from the side and later have the co-ordination to grasp them from the top.

They learn to let go of objects later. At first, children release objects against a hard surface like a table top, the floor or an adult's hand. They later learn to release them into space. They are then able to start placing and posting objects into large containers and as their skills develop they can place them into smaller boxes and tighter holes.

Once able to release objects they learn to start throwing them, at first indiscriminately and later with force and direction.

Fine grasp

Children learn to manipulate and explore toys by handling them, banging them and turning them in all directions.

Their grip becomes more refined as, rather than using their whole hand, they use their thumb and forefinger in the 'pincer grip', thus enabling them to pick up small objects such as raisins, crumbs and pieces of string. This ability to handle small objects will continue to improve over time.

Because they are using their fingers independently, they start to point and prod at things with their forefinger and to tackle posting shapes, stacking bricks and beakers, threading beads onto a string and doing puzzles (inset formboards followed by jigsaws). To begin with, they need to use large equipment which is easy to handle and they will have limited success – for example, stacking only two or three large wooden bricks – but gradually they will be able to stack more and more bricks and of a smaller size.

Using two hands together

Children learn to use both hands together to carry out an activity, for example holding a bowl while scooping food out or pouring from one jug into another.

Twisting

Twisting and turning handles and bottle tops and drinking from a bottle or a cup require wrist control. Children learn to drink from a cup or twist easy knobs quite early but take time to gain the strength to turn large and stiff knobs, the precision to twist small ones and the ability to slide catches.

Undressing and dressing

To undress is easier than to dress (though children do learn fairly early to help when being dressed by putting their arms into sleeves and legs into trousers). First, a child will pull off a hat or a bib, or pull off socks and booties and then shrug off a coat or cardigan. Pulling off pants and trousers follows, then jumpers and shirts. Fastenings, particularly buttons, will be the trickiest element.

Children usually start dressing by putting on easy hats, then cardigans and shirts, followed by pants, trousers and skirts. Socks, shoes and fastenings are the most difficult.

Feeding

Children learn to hold a bottle or lidded cup and drink from it. They gradually become more skilful so that they can use an open cup or beaker without spilling the contents.

Children learn to finger feed themselves with biscuits and pieces of fruit and vegetables, then they learn to feed themselves with a spoon if it is loaded for them and placed conveniently. They then have to learn to scoop the food onto a spoon. This is much easier with foods that stick to the spoon like yoghurt, Weetabix, rice pudding and semolina rather than foods like pasta which just fall off.

Having mastered a spoon, the usual progression is to learn to stab with a fork, then to use a spoon and fork together before finally using a knife and fork (but this would only be developing at school age).

Use of tools

Children learn to use all sorts of different tools which are part of everyday living for adults but require considerable manual skill and dexterity. The usual progression is scooping with spoons and spades, stabbing with forks, cutting with knives, then pincer action with pegs, tongs and scissors.

Using a pencil

Children first grasp a pencil or crayon with their whole fist, then they grip it higher up before the grip changes so that they use fewer fingers and hold it further down. This grip later becomes refined into the adult grip using the thumb and two fingers.

Because drawing and writing are complex skills requiring an intellectual understanding of the marks made, this aspect is included in Chapter 3, pages 53–54.

GAMES AND ACTIVITIES

GROSS MOTOR SKILLS
Chronological development

If your child has a physical disability or wears splints or a special soft helmet at times, check with your physiotherapist or occupational therapist before attempting these activities.

Some children with special needs find any kind of exercise distressing at first and would much rather be left alone. So try making it fun with lots of physical contact between you and your child or make it secure and soothing with music and reassuring talking as you play.

Children who are sensation-impaired have to be watched. If they have no sensation on one side they may get into dangerous situations without being aware of it – they will not be alerted by the pain.

Positions

If you have a baby or a child who is not able to move, make sure that you place him in different positions during the day even if it is only for a short time: Don't always put him in his bouncy cradle or flat on his back in a cot or pram. Each different position encourages a child to use different muscles and see the world in different ways. Try some of the following:

- Place your child on his tummy on a mat on the floor.
- Place your child on his tummy with a rolled-up towel under his chest.
- Lay your child on his side – a particularly good position for playing with toys using both hands together.
- Place your child on his back flat on a mat on the floor.
- Sit on the floor with your legs stretched out in a V shape and place your child on his tummy over your leg either so

that he is in a crawling position with weight through his legs and arms or so that his chest is raised off the ground.

- Sit on the floor with your legs outstretched and sit your baby close to you, between your legs and supported by your body, and looking away from you.

- Sit on the floor with your legs bent and soles of your feet together. Sit your child on the floor, in front of your feet and looking at you. Support him as necessary either with his hands or by his hips.

- Kneel on the floor with your knees apart and sit your child between your legs looking away from you. You can support him by gripping him with your legs.

- Sit on the floor with your legs stretched out in a V shape and sit your child astride your thigh looking at you. This is a

Place your child in different positions

particularly good position if your child wants to push up to standing position.

- Lie on your back and place your child on his tummy on your chest. This is a good position for making eye contact.

- Also try carrying your child in different positions when you move round the house.

Head and neck control

When your child is lying on his back, cradle his shoulders and gradually draw him up into sitting position. Talk to him and make eye contact as you play.

It is also important to do this in reverse, gently getting him to lie back from sitting position.

Weight bearing on forearms

Because of current advice on cot deaths parents are often unwilling to place their children on their tummies during the day, but this position is not dangerous and is, in fact, vital for development. Only place your child on his tummy during the day (not to sleep) and make sure he is constantly supervised.

- Place your child on his tummy on a mat on the floor. A firm surface is best, rather than a soft one like a carrycot. Try different surfaces to make it more interesting, for example carpet, play mats, rugs, sheepskin, wooden floor or lino.

Lay your child on his tummy and place a rolled-up towel under his chest

- Lay him on his tummy and place a rolled-up towel or blanket under his chest so that he lifts his head and shoulders off the ground. This will give him a wider field of vision which he may well enjoy. Alternatively, give him some toys to play with when in this position.

- Lie on the floor and place him on his tummy on your chest. Then encourage him to raise his head and look at your face.

Weight bearing on extended arms

- Place your child on his tummy with a rolled-up blanket or towel under his chest so that his weight is on his elbows. Encourage him to reach for toys like a baby gym with one hand and then the other so that he takes the weight through his arms in turn.

- Lie on the floor on your back and place your child on his tummy on your chest. Use your body to get your child to shift his weight from one arm to the other.

Rolling over

- Lay your child on his back and place one arm above his head out of the way. Gently push the other hip and leg forwards and use a toy as an enticement to get him to roll himself over onto his tummy. Do the same thing on the other side.

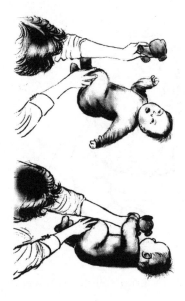

Encouraging your child to roll over

- Roll him halfway and encourage him to continue the roll by placing a favourite toy to one side as an incentive.

- Place him on a rug or pillow and use it to gently rock him from side to side.

Sitting

In order to help a child to sit up you need to practise the gradual pulling up and lowering described in the section on head and neck control (p.127 above) to strengthen all the head, neck and back muscles until he is able to sit alone.

- When he is able to support himself a little in a sitting position, sit him up on your lap and support him by holding his trunk and hips firmly. He will over time need less support.

- Once a child can sit up he needs to develop his balance and strengthen the muscles in his torso. Then he will not fall over at the slightest knock or movement but can reach out to get things and prop (i.e. put his hand and arm out to touch the floor, thereby saving him from falling over).

- When your child is sitting up, put things to his front and side to encourage him to reach out and grasp them and to maintain his balance at the same time.

- When he is sitting gently rock him from side to side and from front to back so that he takes the weight on each side alternately.

- Sit your child astride your thigh, looking at you and rock him sideways to improve his balance. This is particularly good if he has tight muscles around the hips.

- Sit him on a low stool or large firm cushion, hold onto his hips from behind and get him to reach forward for toys and objects.

- When in sitting position put his arms out to his sides, touching the floor and rock him so that he bears weight through his arms and stops himself falling over.

- Sing rowing rhymes with your child like 'Row row row the boat' and 'See-saw Margery Daw'. See Chapter 4, page 96 for the words. Sit on the floor with your child in front of you, hold hands and pretend to row backwards and forwards.

- Going on swings, rocking horses or other bouncy and rocking toys are all good exercise for strengthening the torso.

- Horse riding (through the Riding for the Disabled Association) is also extremely good for strengthening the body and for balance since every movement of the horse encourages the child to make a compensatory movement. It is particularly good for children who have tight muscles since they have to open up their hips on a horse.

- If muscle tightness is a problem, encourage your child to sit in a cross-legged position and not in the W position where he sits between splayed legs. This is also a good idea if he has a tendency to roll in on his ankles.

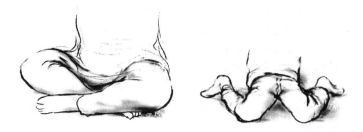

Crossed legs and W position

Crawling

Crawling is a very important skill to learn as bearing weight through shoulders and arms is vital for later skills using hands and arms. Parents are often anxious to move children onto walking as early as possible, but in fact children should be allowed to move on in their own good time.

It is important that children learn four-point or reciprocal crawling where they move one leg and the opposite arm together, rather than bunny crawling, which is where they bring both legs up together.

- Hold your child on his front, supporting his tummy and fly him through the air. This will extend his back.

- Place your child, tummy down, over an inflatable roll with his hands and knees touching the floor. Then rock him backwards and forwards so that he takes the weight alternately through his arms and hips.

- Place your child in crawling position and rock him backwards and forwards in order to give him the idea of crawling and to get him to start taking some of his weight on his arms and knees.

- Pass a towel under your child's tummy and chest and then hold it firmly above him. You can then lift his torso off the ground, while leaving his arms and legs in contact with the floor and get him to simulate crawling while you support his weight.

Encouraging the crawling position

- Children usually learn to crawl backwards before going forwards because their arms are stronger than their legs. Once your child is crawling backwards you can be confident that he will eventually move forwards. However, if you want to help him, place him on all fours with his feet against a hard surface – the sofa, wall or your hands and encourage him to move forwards.

- When he is in the crawling position tempt him forwards with favourite toys just out of reach. Be careful not to make him too frustrated.

- Once he is crawling give him lots of practice by playing chasing games round the house.

High kneeling

Before trying to get your child to stand get him to balance on his knees. It will be much easier for him to bear weight through half the length of his legs than the whole length and it will strengthen and develop his hips.

High kneeling position

- Place him in an upright kneeling position against a low table or a sofa on which there are toys to play with.

- When he is in kneeling position push him gently from side to side so that he has to regain his balance.

High stride kneeling

From the high kneeling position place one of his feet flat on the ground and draw him up with all his weight over his foot.

Standing

- Kneel on the floor facing a chair or sofa. Sit your child on your knees facing away from you and with his feet flat on the floor, rise up, raising your bottom off your ankles, and thereby lift your child into the standing position supporting him around the pelvis.

- Fix bars, for instance the side of an old cot, to a wall and attach interesting toys to encourage your child to pull himself up to standing using the bars.

- Cut the legs down on a small chair so that your child can place his feet flat on the ground when sitting down. Place the chair in front of some bars on a wall and encourage him to stand up.

- Holding your child's hands get him to stand up from a squatting position and then return again. This will help strengthen his leg muscles.

- Put toys on a sofa or low table and stand your child against it either with you behind him to give support or alone if he can support himself and encourage your child to play while standing. Some children will need to use a standing frame to do this (provided by physiotherapists).

- When he is in a standing position, push him gently so that he is forced to regain his balance.

- Stand your child against a wall or in a corner and play a game with him, for instance banging a tambourine or playing with a ball.

Cruising

Once he is able to stand try to get your child to cruise around the furniture using appropriate enticements like favourite toys. Create an environment where chairs, sofas and low tables are placed close enough for him to cruise easily.

Walking

- When your child is standing against the furniture, lift one of his legs off the ground to encourage weight bearing on the other leg.

- Once he is cruising, any kind of sturdy truck or trolley to push around will help him get the idea of putting one foot in front of the other.

- While your child is learning to walk it is important that he is supported from the front and at his hand height. Being hauled along from behind, gripped under the armpits, gives the wrong posture.

- Check with your physiotherapist to see if it is appropriate to use a baby-walker. They are not suitable for children who have muscle-tightness problems or are at all floppy and they are generally not liked by physiotherapists because they do not actually reproduce the walking motion. Children are supported in them and paddle their legs. On the other hand, used for short periods only and with constant supervision, they may be helpful in giving a child the idea of using his legs to move.

- Place your child on a push-along toy like a small tricycle or a car and push him round the garden. This is good for giving him the opportunity to push through his legs and gives the idea of movement.

- Place your child with his back to a wall and get him to hold an object which you also hold. Then encourage him to walk forward. A hoop is perfect for this since your child can hold the back and you the front.

Balance

Once a child has learnt to walk further physical development is generally reliant on a good sense of balance.

- Put your child in a large cardboard box and drag him around the room so that he has to balance as he is moved about.

- Get your child to step over small obstacles like a low wall made out of bricks, a plank of wood, door thresholds, a rope or sticks.

- Get your child to walk on a narrow beam, a low wall, a plank of wood or a thick line that you have drawn on the ground.

- Build stepping stones from bricks, upturned terracotta flower pots, slabs, mats or paint pots and get your child to walk on them.

- Get your child to stand on one leg.

- When you are in the baby pool or shallow end of a swimming pool where he can stand upright, get your child to do different things. For example, get him to walk, run, throw a ball, pour water or play with floats. He will have to work hard in the water to maintain his balance.

- Play throwing games; for example, throw balls to each other or into a box or bucket or play skittles. Throwing a ball affects balance and a child has to learn to compensate in order not to fall over.

- Play any racquet games where your child has to get to the ball and balance as he hits it with his racquet.

- Try kicking games; for example, kick a ball between you and your child, and get him to try to score a goal or dribble round obstacles. This requires a good sense of balance as your child has to balance on one leg and kick with the other.

Agility

- Play hide and seek games.

- Play chase or 'it' games.

- Get him to play on equipment in playgrounds or at a children's gym session.

- Encourage your child to do somersaults, where there is a soft landing. But check with your physiotherapist first.

- Create your own playgrounds inside and outside. If you allow it, turn your sitting room into a soft play area for an afternoon, where children can climb over sofas, crawl through tunnels, jump off low tables, do somersaults on cushions, climb into boxes and crawl under chairs.

Flexibility

- In the swimming pool support your child when he is lying on his back and get him to kick his legs. This is good for flexibility in the legs and hips.

- Play hopscotch and other skipping and hopping games.

- Play 'Simon Says' and 'Here we go round the mulberry bush'. This is a good way of practising physical skills like stretching, bending and turning in a non-confrontational way. For example, you can say 'This is the way we touch our toes' or 'Simon Says stretch up high'.

Jumping

- Get your child to jump on a trampoline. A small one with a handle for him to hold as he bounces is particularly suitable.

- Encourage your child to jump off a step or, if swimming, off the side into the pool with an adult ready to catch him. You could use the Humpty Dumpty rhyme as a prompt. Encourage your child to bend his knees.

- Find low steps, such as the bottom step of a flight of stairs, logs or low walls, for your child to jump off.

Running

Running comes gradually as children gain confidence to speed up their walking. Give your child lots of opportunities to run around outside in a safe environment and, in particular, play chasing games to encourage him to speed up.

Climbing up and down

Children start climbing soon after they start crawling. Start with low, easy climbs – onto a low stool or sofa. Use a favourite toy as motivation.

To show your child how to climb off a sofa or bed safely, place him on his tummy and get him to slide down backwards, moving his legs and arms in sequence. This will show him how to get down feet first.

Spatial awareness

Children need to learn where they are and where their limbs are in relation to other objects and the ground. By learning spatial awareness they learn how to move around objects safely without colliding into them, and when it is safe to jump off something high up.

- Provide opportunities to climb through, over and under objects for example tunnels, stiles, tables, large boxes and chairs. Play hide and seek games and encourage your child to hide in narrow, confined spaces. Soft play areas and playgrounds with climbing frames are good for this.

- Play with hoops as they are extremely useful for learning about spatial awareness. Put one over your child's head, get him to climb through it or draw it over him.

- Label spatial terms as you play – top of the slide, under the chair or through the hoop.

- Play games which encourage an awareness of body image. For example ask your child to become as small as a mouse, as big as a house, make a star shape, etc.

- Swimming provides an opportunity for your child to feel where he is in the water.

- Horse riding, as in Riding for the Disabled, is useful because children are in a different position to normal. They have to be aware of the position of their limbs and where the ground is in relation to them.

Rhythm

Children need to gain a natural rhythm to their movements and good co-ordination. Moving and performing actions to music is very helpful.

- Clap and sway to music with different beats.

- Listen to music and move appropriately; for example, march, gallop, creep and tip-toe.

- Dance to music of all kinds. If your child is not walking, you can encourage him to move to the music with his arms and torso or, if he is sitting down, to swing his legs freely in time to the music. Try all sorts of music from pop to jazz to classical.

Foot–eye co-ordination

Encourage your child to do the following activities which all improve foot–eye co-ordination:

- Kick a ball at targets using the left leg and then the right

- Dribble a ball round obstacles
- Run to the left, stop and then run to the right
- Jump on the spot then to the left, the right, forwards and backwards
- Hop on the left leg then the right leg
- Play hopscotch and skipping
- Do trampolining
- Climb ladders.

Parallel development
Physical play

It is important for children to have a chance to experience lively physical play. You need to gauge what is appropriate for your child. Give him the chance to enjoy the sensation of movement but make sure he is feeling comfortable and confident by holding him securely and talking to him. Only take it as far as your child wants, never force it.

In addition, whatever your child's special needs, it is important not to be over-protective. Give him the opportunity to practise physical skills and thereby gain confidence. If your child is delayed it can be alarming to see him falling over, since he is much bigger and therefore has further to fall, but it is important that he has the chance to play. Playgrounds, soft play sessions, sand pits, beaches and gardens are good, relatively safe environments.

- Hold your child close to you and swing him round and round; tip him upside down and swing him by his ankles. Take your cue from your child and be as gentle or as rough as is appropriate.
- Dance to music while holding your child.
- Play roly poly by laying your child on the bed, holding him around the shoulders or by the hands and rocking him. Alternatively, put his head and shoulders on a pillow and rock him with the pillow.
- Attend soft play sessions with soft equipment to climb up, down, under and over. Many recreation centres and private

Dance to music holding your child

organizations run classes or sessions for young children to
play on bouncy castles, ball ponds and soft equipment.

- Attend gym courses for young children. In a safe and
controlled environment children can learn to climb and jump
and to experiment with simple gym equipment such as
beams and trampolines.

Riding for the Disabled

There are many Riding for the Disabled groups throughout the
country as well as more specialist organizations which provide
riding therapy for children with special needs.

Riding has two major benefits for children with special needs.
First, it is extremely good exercise. If you don't ride you probably
won't appreciate that the rider has to make compensatory
movements constantly for the motion of the horse. It can also be
used to encourage specific physical developments at every stage,
for example strengthening the trunk, improving head control,
establishing the prop reflex, replicating the walking motion,

Riding

balance and spatial awareness. Second, interacting with horses can be very rewarding in emotional terms for children with special needs because it can offer a stimulating and joyful experience and perhaps provide a rare motivation. Riding also enables children who are not mobile to move around.

Usually a weekly riding session lasts for about 15–20 minutes. Children are led and side-walked by volunteers, as considered necessary. The session typically involves different exercises and games on horseback.

Swimming

Swimming can be a wonderful activity for children with special needs but only if the person who takes them is confident in the water. Your child will pick up on any nervousness and hesitancy on the part of the adult.

The main purpose of playing in a swimming pool at this age is to have fun. Any kind of playing, splashing, kicking and jumping in a pool is beneficial since it will improve muscle control and flexibility. In the water you have to work harder and yet you are supported. For children with a physical disability it can give a great sense of freedom and equality.

Be careful that your child does not get too cold in the water. Some children feel the cold more than others, especially if they are not very active in the pool. If, on the other hand, the water is very warm children may tire very quickly.

If your child is frightened of going in the water, introduce him very gradually. Begin perhaps by letting him watch from the side, then get him to sit on the side and splash; later get him to play with someone in the water, perhaps with a ball or jugs. Only when he is ready bring him into the water properly. Sometimes it is worth approaching the pool from a different angle, perhaps by walking around the pool and going in from the other end. Many pools have attractive murals on the walls; use these as a distraction.

Swimming

Sometimes swimming pools can be very noisy which can frighten children, so if possible choose a quiet time or attend a special session for people with disabilities; such sessions tend to be quieter than public sessions.

Some pools run water confidence courses for children from three months upwards. These show how to handle your child in the water and give ideas for games.

The following are ideas for things you can easily do in the swimming pool:

- Get your child to splash you with his legs and arms and make a big game of it by giggling, laughing, making silly faces and pretending to be upset to encourage him to do more. This is very good for strengthening muscles and for flexibility.

- Push a ball to and fro between you to strengthen his arms.

- Play jumping kangaroos. Hold your child's hands and get him to jump up and down in the water to strengthen his legs.

- Blow bubbles in the water. This is good for strengthening muscles in the throat and encouraging different sounds.

- Get your child to throw a ball to you, it will push him off balance and he will have to learn to correct himself.

- Hold your child and play 'Ring a ring o' roses', falling down in the water. You can go under water when your child is ready.

- Sit or stand your child on the side of the swimming pool, sing 'Humpty Dumpty' and get him to jump in.

FINE MOTOR SKILLS
Chronological development

For all fine motor skills the position of the child is crucial. If he is badly positioned he will not be able to do many of the things described below. Always consider the position of your child (see Chapter 2, pp.34–35). If your child has physical disabilities which make positioning difficult, consult your occupational therapist for advice.

If your child has a visual impairment it is a good idea to keep toys in a box or on a tray so that he can find them with confidence.

Encouraging use of hands

For children who have a problem with muscle control in their hands, it is very important to encourage them to use their hands as much as possible so that they build up their muscle control and dexterity. The following games will encourage your child to open up his hand and use his fingers.

- Try playing with different substances and get your child to handle them in all sorts of ways – feeling, patting, poking, stroking and pulling.
- Play with sand both wet and dry or peat.
- Play with water (sometimes with bubbles, food colouring or fairy flakes).
- Play with play dough.

Play dough recipe

2 cups plain flour
2 cups water
1 cup salt
4 tbsp cream of tartar
4 tbsp oil
food colouring

Place all the ingredients in a saucepan and stir over a gentle heat until it reaches the right consistency. The play dough will keep for some time if kept in an airtight container in the fridge.

- Make up cornflour mixed with water. This has an amazing quality. It looks hard but feels soft and can be stretched into strings and different shapes.
- You can cook some extra spaghetti and let your child play with it when cold.
- Also try shaving foam and face cream, especially those brands which contain rough textured bits.
- Look at books which incorporate different textures and get your child to feel the surfaces.
- Get your child to mix cake dough and pastry with his hands.

- Play with the following materials: tin foil, bubble wrap, old newspapers and magazines, fabrics including carpet and furnishing material, soft balls, cotton wool and Koosh balls.

- Play with musical toys.

- Do some finger painting.

- Play splashing games in the bath or swimming pool.

- Do the 'Round and round the garden' rhyme. It will open up the palm of his hand.

- In a swimming pool get your child to push a ball to you on the surface of the water and keep it going to and fro between you.

- Put small sponges in the bath and get your child to pick them up and squeeze the water out.

Batting

- Place light rattles in your child's hand or try wrist rattles or bells sewn on gloves to encourage him to move his hands.

- Place objects on a piece of string across a pram, cot, pushchair or bouncy cradle or use a baby gym. These keep toys within easy reach. They can be used if the child is able to sit or still lies on his back. Tie different toys on to give variety and change them regularly so he does not get bored. Try anything which is strongly coloured and likely to catch his eye, for example bells, shiny paper, pictures, rattles, mirrors, beads, unbreakable Christmas decorations and keys. Also things which make a good noise. Even yoghurt pots and bottle tops make a good sound when tied together on a piece of string.

Grasping

Play with:

- bean bags covered in a variety of textures and with different fillings like beans, buttons, pasta and coins;

- soft blocks which are easy to grasp;

- small rattles, teething rings and hoops;

- pieces of dowel (a good size is 4 x 0.5in (10 x 1.25cm) diameter) covered in different textures such as silver foil, fur, velvet and bubble wrap.

Placing and releasing

- Get your child to release the object he is holding against a hard surface or your hands.

- Encourage your child to drop objects from a height so they make a nice bang. You could place a cake tin or box by his high chair and drop objects into it. Tie objects onto a piece of string so he can retrieve them and drop them again.

- Get him to place objects in a large shallow container, preferably one that makes a loud noise. Tins or small swing top plastic bins are good for this. Gradually reduce the size of the opening.

- Post objects like ping-pong balls in formula milk bottle tins by cutting a large hole in the top and making it smaller as your child progresses.

- Place a large object on top of another, for instance a toy car on an upturned cake tin, and knock it off noisily. To begin with use easily grasped, smallish objects placed on top of large ones. As your child progresses reduce the size of all the objects. For example, use wooden, plastic or soft bricks to build towers.

- Get him to transfer objects from one container to another.

- Throw and roll balls to your child and encourage him to return them.

- Place bean bags into a hoop, balls into a bucket or other objects into a box or basket.

- Get your child to feed himself with pieces of fruit, vegetables, toast, crisps or biscuits.

- Encourage your child to help you tidy up toys and place them in the correct box.

Pointing

Having strength in the index finger is important for fine motor skills, in particular writing.

- Get your child to play with piano keyboards, press doorbells or switches.

- Point out pictures in a book. Ask 'Where's the bicycle?' type questions and get your child to point to the picture. Also point to people in photographs.

- Look at noisy books where your child has to press a button to hear the sound.

- Play with any toys with buttons to press, for example pop-up type toys, cash registers, press-and-go cars and tape recorders.

- Do finger painting with your child.

- Get him to dial using an old-fashioned telephone.

- Encourage him to pop bubbles with one finger.

- Get him to draw on steamy windows or in wet and dry sand.

- Play with play dough or pastry when cooking and get your child to poke his finger into the dough to make holes.

- Play at flicking marbles and ping-pong balls.

- Play with finger puppets.

> Dan likes putting his finger in my mouth. As a game I close my mouth suddenly and catch his finger before he can take it away. It's good for his eye contact too.

Fine grasp

As a general rule start with light objects that easily fit in the hand and then gradually introduce heavier, smaller and larger ones.

- Play at building towers with bricks, beakers, household objects, Duplo, coins and buttons.

- Get your child to place things like Duplo, cotton reels, bricks and buttons in boxes and containers.

- Draw and cut out pictures of small animals like ducks, fish or frogs and draw a pond on a piece of paper. Get your child to place the animals in the pond.

- Draw an outline shape of a car or a dog and get your child to place shiny stickers inside the shape. You can glue yarn to the outline to make a raised edge.

- Play with fuzzy felts and sticker books.

- Play posting games, for example:
  - Place shapes in a shape sorter. Whistling and noisy shape sorters are particularly popular. Make your own shape sorter with different shapes cut into the lid of a formula milk tin.

- Run cars, balls or marbles down marble runs or old cardboard tubes (from cling film or wrapping paper).

- Use everyday activities like posting letters in a letter box, putting tapes in a tape recorder, putting books on a bookshelf, plates in a plate rack, cutlery in a tray, money in a piggy bank, toy till or charity box.

- Do puzzles – inset form boards or conventional jigsaw puzzles. It is often very difficult to motivate children to do puzzles because they are not terribly interesting or rewarding, so look out for pictures which might stimulate your child. Duplo or other pull apart toys may be more interesting. Alternatively, try fitting together train tracks.

- Get your child to put clothes pegs around the edge of a cardboard box or pinch off pieces of play dough or Bluetack.

- Encourage him to pick up small pieces of food such as peas, raisins, dried fruit, crisps, Smarties, chocolate buttons and hundreds and thousands.

- Get him to thread large beads with a thick and stiff piece of cord (washing line is very good to begin with), then move onto smaller beads and buttons and flimsier cord and eventually a shoe lace.

- Get him to place tops on pens, bottles and jars.

- Play with wind-up toys.

Twisting

Get your child to do the following:

- Twist bottle tops, jar lids, door handles, control knobs on children's tape recorders and pop-up toys with twisting knobs.

- Spin balls and tops.

- Turn over cards in memory games.

Encouraging two-handedness

Though most people have a preference for one hand, children have to have strength and control in both hands to do two-handed tasks. Encourage activities which require two hands and if your child has a weak side, play games to strengthen that.

Encourage two-handedness with water play

- Start by getting your child to move an object from one hand to the other in order to pick up another toy. So give your child one toy and then another and rather than let him just drop the first, get him to transfer it to his other hand. For example, two drum beaters to bang on a drum, two bricks to bang together, a cup and then a spoon to put in.

- Offer a toy directly in front of your child so that he can use either hand to take it. If you are trying to encourage one hand specifically, offer the toy on that side of him.

- Play with water or sand using buckets, funnels, jugs, sieves and cups and encourage your child to pour from one to another.

- Catch and throw a large ball, or roll a large ball between you when sitting on the floor.

- Use play dough – rolling with a rolling pin, or patting with two hands.

- Get your child to hold his bowl or plate with one hand while he feeds himself with the other.

- Play with pull-apart toys like Duplo or Stickle Bricks.

- When cooking get your child to stir the bowl and hold it at the same time.

- Encourage your child to bath or feed dolls, later progressing to dressing them.

- Play musical instruments like the tambourine, finger cymbals or hand-held drum.

- Play with screwing toys from a tool set.

- Get your child to pull tops off bottles and pens and unscrew toothpaste tubes then put them back again.

- Encourage your child to clap, for example by clapping to music or by singing songs like 'Pat-a-cake', 'Wind the bobbin up' or 'Five fat sausages' (see Chapter 3, p.59 and p.70 for words).

- Get your child to clap bubbles to pop them.

- Play at threading beads onto a lace.

- Encourage your child to tear paper into thin strips by holding the paper with one hand and tearing with the other.

- Make a toy unsteady so that your child has to hold it steady with one hand while playing with the other.

If your child has a specific weakness on one side:

- Put cot toys and bath toys on the weaker side.

- Place a fork and spoon in each hand even if your child tends to feed with just one.

- Place or offer toys to his weaker side to encourage him to pick them up and play with them with the weaker hand or at least pass them across to his stronger hand.

- Give your child a malleable substance like a soft ball, cotton wool or play dough to manipulate in the weaker hand.

- Put a sock or mitten over the stronger hand and encourage your child to pull it off with the weaker hand.

Shoulder strengthening to aid hand control

Weight bearing through the shoulders and hands is very important because you need strength and control in your shoulders and arms before you can attempt delicate movements with your hands.

- Play wheelbarrows with your child. If he cannot support himself on his arms alone support him under his hips.

- Encourage your child to crawl through tunnels and narrow places.

- Get your child on all fours and then, while he maintains that position, play games that he enjoys like marbles, puzzles or card games.

- Get your child to kneel on all fours and stretch out his left leg and right arm and balance. Repeat using the opposite arm and leg.

- Get your child to do push-ups from his tummy.

Crawling through tunnels strengthens the shoulders

Tool use

Pen control

Use crayons, pencils or pens which are easy for your child to hold. Chunky pens are better than thin ones and triangular shapes are good. Use ones which make good clear marks so that your child gets an instant reward for his effort rather than pens which have to be held at a particular angle to work.

It is good to get children to work on an easel or wall because it makes them open up their wrist in a good writing position, whereas if they are working on a flat surface they can keep their wrists very bent. Try chalking, painting, drawing, colouring or fuzzy felt games.

Try any games which encourage your child to enjoy making marks on paper or other surfaces, for example:

- make patterns in sand (wet and dry);
- put sand on coloured paper and move it around;
- finger painting;
- chalking.

For further ideas of games for writing and colouring see Chapter 3, pages 72–75.

Scooping

- Get your child to practise scooping with sand (both wet and dry).
- Allow him to use a spoon to transfer rice or pulses from one container to another.
- Get your child to scoop washing powder when you are loading the washing machine.
- Let your child dig in the garden or fill pots with soil.
- Try different cooking activities like dolloping spoonfuls of cake mixture into a tin or into individual pastry cases.

Pouring

- During water play or in the bath give your child lots of jugs, beakers, empty bottles, funnels and water mills so that he can practise pouring. Do the same with dry sand in a sand pit if you have one or in a bucket on a plastic sheet if you don't.
- Take turns watering flowers and pots with a watering can or jug.

Tongs

Use kitchen tongs to pick up objects (the movement is a useful preparation to using scissors because it requires a pincer grip).

Cutting with scissors

There are lots of different types of scissors to experiment with. Some are two-handed so that the parent uses the scissors behind the child to give the idea of squeezing and releasing. Others are called loop scissors and have a spring action so that the child only has to squeeze and not release.

You can borrow these from your portage home visitor, occupational therapist or playgroup to see if they can help before you buy them since they are only available from specialist suppliers.

- Get your child to practise using tongs first and to squeeze sponges because these require a similar movement.

- Start by giving your child light card rather than paper because this will be easier to cut. Cut long narrow strips so that he can cut across them and immediately see the strips cut in half. Gradually increase the width so that he has to make more and more snips.

- Draw thick lines for your child to cut along – initially straight lines, then with bends and then slight curves.

- Once your child can cut try different craft activities with him like cutting up pictures in magazines and old catalogues to make collages. Try cutting up old Christmas cards and birthday cards to make new ones, folding up a piece of paper and cutting holes to make snowflake pictures, and cutting and sticking coloured paper to make mosaics.

Using a fork

Get your child to stab food with a fork and practise this with play dough.

Cutting with a knife

Give your child a blunt knife to cut play dough into 'sausages'.

Parallel development
Feeding

If your child is having problems feeding himself it is worth experimenting with different equipment. There is a wide range of cups, bowls and angled spoons and forks on the market. If this does not work, ask your occupational therapist for advice and for the loan of more specialist equipment. Speech therapists will help with problems to do with muscle control such as chewing.

If you are working on improving feeding, don't try to do too much at once. Aim to improve feeding skills during one course of each meal and then let your child finger-feed the others. Alternatively, start off by taking time with the first half dozen

mouthfuls and then allow your child to eat how he wants and gradually extend the time spent eating 'properly'.

Finger feeding

Give your child pieces of food such as breadsticks, biscuits, cooked vegetables and fruit which are easily chewed to establish the idea of taking food to the mouth.

Using a spoon

Load the spoon and get the child to take it to his mouth. Use the hand-over-hand method initially and then reduce the prompt as your child improves. Try an angled spoon to make it easier.

When he is taking the spoon to his mouth successfully, get him to replace the spoon in the bowl.

Scooping with a spoon for feeding

Move on to getting your child to scoop food onto his spoon.

- Start with food which is easy to scoop such as yoghurt, thick soups and stews rather than food which is likely to drop off a spoon such as pasta.

- Play with your child at scooping with sand, water and other materials (see above under Scooping, p.151).

- Try placing a non-slip mat under the bowl or using a bowl with a suctioned bottom so that the bowl remains stuck to the table top and does not move around.

- Use bowls with near vertical sides rather than shallow ones with gradually sloping sides because they make it easier for the child to scoop.

Stabbing with a fork

Find opportunities for your child to use a fork, for example when eating food such as melon, pasta, cooked carrot, lumps of potato and meat.

Using a spoon and fork

Once your child can use a fork or a spoon introduce both together.

Dressing and undressing

Problems with dressing and undressing are often linked to a physical difficulty which is highly specific and which requires an approach geared to each individual child. In such a case you need to consult your occupational therapist. If, on the other hand, your child finds dressing difficult because of delayed or poor fine motor skills rather than a specific physical disability the following ideas may help.

Think of your child's position. Make him sit down to dress or undress. He will find it easier to concentrate on the process itself when he does not have to worry about supporting himself and keeping his balance as he moves around.

- Play dressing-up in adult clothes.

- Practise dressing during the day as a game when there is no time pressure. In the morning you are often in a hurry to get on and get out and in the evenings children are often tired and irritable.

- Break all skills down into small achievable tasks.

- Use backward and forward chaining techniques as described in Chapter 2, pages 36–87.

- Make up fastenings, for example zips, Velcro and buttons and stick them on boards which are solid and do not move around, then get your child to practise doing and undoing the fastenings.

Hand–eye co-ordination

If a child has poor hand–eye co-ordination, use any or all of the above activities which practise fine motor skills. These will all assist progress in this area.

CHAPTER 6

Sensory Development

VISION

Vision is the most important of the senses in terms of development as it affects so much of how and what we learn. There is a strong interplay between vision and our ability to handle objects and to understand the world about us.

Newborn babies focus on faces more than anything else and specifically on those which are close to them, about eight to ten inches away, the distance between a baby and her parent when being fed. Given a range of different things to look at, a baby will choose a face. Babies are aware of vague shapes and dark and light and find patterns more interesting than solid areas.

Having learnt to focus on faces nearby, babies then learn to track objects, following them with their eyes as they move.

They then gradually develop the ability to see further and further away – up to a couple of feet, to the other side of the room, and so on. Ultimately they have an adult range of vision.

Children use their sight to develop an understanding of object permanence (that people and things continue to exist even if they cannot be seen). This is covered in greater detail in Chapter 3, page 50, because it is crucial to children's understanding of the world and the way it works.

They then use their vision to gain an awareness of space, of where their bodies are in space and of how they can use what they see. For example, they learn that if they are sitting down and about to topple over, they can put their arms out to save themselves. They are thereby showing that they understand that the floor is a horizontal plane.

They also start to use their understanding of what they see in their interaction with other people. At a basic level they use it for eye contact, turn-taking, and picking up on body language. Later they will use the information in their relations with others. For example if they see a toy at the other side of the room and someone else is nearby they ask that person to get it for them.[1]

HEARING

Babies' hearing and understanding of what they hear and where it comes from develops with age. Newborn babies are startled by sudden noises. They show this by responding to a loud noise with the Moro or startle reflex – throwing their arms back and widening their eyes.

They become interested in human voices and their mother's in particular. If they are content they will quieten, turn and listen to a voice talking or singing. If they are screaming for a feed, however, they are not likely to take much notice.

Children then start listening to all sorts of sounds such as the vacuum cleaner whining or the tap running. They show excitement at certain sounds and sometimes will turn to sounds made close by. They also start to discriminate between the sounds they hear so that, for instance, they eventually recognize the noise made by the washing machine or a car engine.

Children then start to respond to the human voice with coos and gurgles, i.e. to take turns in 'conversations'. As they listen to sounds they try to work out where they are coming from. Usually they locate sounds with one ear before the other.

Gradually they get better at locating sounds. Initially they locate sounds made near them, for example a noisy rattle shaken nearby. Later they start to locate and recognize noises made

---

[1]   See Sonksen, P.M. and Levitt, S. (1984) 'Identification of constraints acting on motor development in young, physically disabled children and principles of remediation.' *Child Care, Health and Development 10*, 273–286. See also Sheridan, M.D. (1977) *Spontaneous Play in Early Childhood*. London: Routledge; Sonksen, P.M. (1983) *Vision and Early Development: Paediatric Opthalmology* (pp.85–95); Sonksen, P.M. (1984) 'A developmental approach to sensory disabilities in early childhood.' *International Rehabilitation Medicine 7*, 27–32; and Sonksen, P.M. (1991) 'Promotion of visual development in severely visually impaired babies.' *Developmental Medicine and Child Neurology 33*, 320–335.

further away within the room and then beyond, like a door bell ringing and later an aeroplane flying overhead.

Children have to listen in order to process the sounds that they hear and to understand that certain sounds are words and have meaning, i.e. that they are listening to speech.

We live in very noisy environments with a constant background of sound such as the hum of traffic, birds singing, clocks ticking and washing machines whirring. Children therefore also have to learn to screen out all the irrelevant noises and focus on the important sounds like the person talking to them.

Children first hear high-frequency noises, which is why adults tend to talk to babies in high sing-songy voices and babies respond better to women's voices. As their hearing develops they become able to hear lower frequencies too.

TASTE

Children are born with a liking for sweet foods. In fact, breast milk tastes sweet. Children then acquire a taste for savoury foods as they are introduced to them.

Children's tastes are largely established by the age of 15 months. So a child who has been given only sweet foods such as fruit purées will maintain a preference for them. It is important therefore that young children are exposed to as wide a variety of tastes and textures as possible at a young age. Even if they show a preference for one particular taste, others should be introduced.

GAMES AND ACTIVITIES

VISION
General advice for children with visual impairment

- Give your child a running commentary of what you are doing in simple language so she can understand what is going on.

- Use the same words for the same activities, to give warning of what is going to happen, and then develop the idea of language by association.

- Talk to your child gently before approaching to give her warning and to avoid startling or frightening her.

- Place toys on a tray so that your child can locate them and keep them contained. Once she is used to the position, move them around so she develops the idea of object permanence and improves her feeling skills.

- Use a babygym so your child can touch toys without stretching.

Stimulating looking

Children with a visual impairment usually have some vision and it is important that they learn to use well what vision they have. Therefore try to stimulate what vision there is as much as possible. Children with special needs other than a visual impairment may also need encouragement to look at things and reach for them.

The RNIB advises parents of children with visual impairment:

- big toys are best – fiddly little toys are difficult to see and handle;

- colourful toys are easier to see – eyes work on contrasts so start with black and white then move on to colours like red and yellow; fluorescent colours are also good as is shiny and holographic paper;

- a bright well-lit environment is best.[2]

Use visually exciting materials

Newborn and young babies can only see a very short distance so that any pictures or objects must be placed very close to the baby, about ten inches away initially. Mobiles, however colourful, will not be seen unless they are really close to the child.

Babies are fascinated by faces so find or draw pictures of faces for your child to look at and stick them on the sides of her cot.

The following are also likely to stimulate interest and encourage a child to look:

- glittery, shiny, silver or holographic paper covering objects;

- lights – torches shone round the room and on holographic paper, fairy lights, books and toys with flashing lights, fibre-optic torches available from joke shops and fun fairs;

- shiny objects which catch and reflect light;

2   See RNIB and Play Matters/NATLL (1987) *Look and Touch*.

- mirrors;
- hard, shiny toys rather than soft, furry ones;
- tactile toys with interesting textures to feel;
- spare keys;
- balloons;
- metallic toy windmills;
- musical toys.

Find an organization with a sensory room which your child could use. Sensory rooms are designed to provide maximum stimulation of the senses in a fun, educational or therapeutic way. They use music, textures, aromas and, particularly, lights – especially fibre-optics.

> I'll never forget when I took Natasha into the sensory room when she was six months old. She hadn't really responded to anything visually before, but I brought a 'spray' of fibre-optic lights towards her face and she suddenly startled back, as if she'd seen something for the first time. Well, that was it. We bought loads of fancy flashing torches and lights to stimulate her vision. I am sure it helped, because now she has learnt to use what little vision she has without the need for flashing lights.

Use other senses

Use activities which engage each of the other senses to encourage a child to look, such as the following.

SOUND

- Hide squeaky toys.
- Sing and recite nursery rhymes with actions.
- Play with musical toys and instruments.
- Hang up wind-chimes around the house.

It is good to use noisy toys. If possible find toys with different sounds so that your child can recognize objects by the sound they make. If your child hears a noise, she needs to see or touch the source of it so that she learns the importance and meaning of sounds. If she does not she may learn to ignore sounds.

TEXTURE

Gather objects from around the house for your child to play with. You could make a lucky dip bin. Children's toys seem to be predominantly primary-coloured plastic, yet children need to explore other weights, textures and qualities. Use candles, wooden spoons, saucepan lids, metal spoons, cardboard, cellophane, tissue paper, inserts from chocolate boxes and biscuit tins, sponges or fabrics (silk, fur, sequins, leather, carpet, sandpaper or furnishing fabrics).

TASTE

All children explore with their mouths because it is the most sensitive part of the body.

SMELL

Use aromatherapy oils mixed with cream and spread some on her hands and feet. Exaggerate the act of smelling them and bring them to her nose. Also use horrible smells like onion.

Tracking objects

- Attach a balloon to a piece of string and pin it to a door frame or the ceiling and bat it for your child to follow it with your eyes.

- Push friction cars so that they move slowly across the floor. Ones with flashing lights or moving parts are particularly good.

- Roll a ball in front of your child. A brightly coloured one with a bell inside is ideal.

- Move a squeaky toy across your child's field of vision and get her to follow it with her eyes.

- When your child is in her highchair, move a toy around the outside edge of the tray so that she follows it with her eyes.

Tracking an object

- Get your child to throw a soft ball at a target on the wall, in a net or in a box.

HEARING

General guidelines

When talking to your child, make sure you are near her and in front of her. Get her attention, make sure she can see your face and make eye contact. This is particularly important if your child has a hearing impairment.

Encouraging listening

- Focus on the noises that things make.

- When looking at books or playing with toys, ask: 'What noise does the cow make? Moo.' Talk about the dog, car, the bicycle, aeroplane etc.

- Play with noisy toys with different beeps, bells and sounds. It is also quite easy to fill plastic bottles and containers with different things to make different sounds – rice, pasta, beans, buttons, water etc.

- Go round the house listening to the noises made by different household objects like the fridge, washing machine, doorbell, vacuum cleaner, taps and clocks.

Go on listening walks

- Go on listening walks. Outside the house point out noises such as the birds, the rustle of leaves, rain, fountains and traffic.

- There are tapes available where you match pictures to sounds. Alternatively, you can make up your own by recording noises around the house (washing machine, dog, clock, blender, doorbell) or in the vicinity (cars, rain, birdsong) and take your own photographs to go with them.

- Play listening lotto. Each of you should have a lotto board. Make a pile of the individual cards and say what each picture shows; get your child to call out if it is on her board. The first person to complete her board is the winner.

- Ready, steady, go games encourage a child to listen for the all important signal to start.

Locating sounds

- Talk to your child as you walk in and out of the room she is in to get her to pick up on where the sound is coming from.

- Hide a noisy toy under the tray of your child's highchair and get her to locate it.

- Play games to find a noisy toy, for instance hide a radio or clock which ticks loudly and get your child to find it. Alternatively, you can hide any toy and then make louder noises as your child gets nearer and quieter noises as she gets further away from it.

- Focus on the noises that you hear in the house or coming from outside and with your child try to find where they are coming from. For example, listen out for and locate the washing machine, the door bell, the coffee machine, the helicopter, etc.

Musical games

Musical activities are very good for listening and concentration and also for timing and anticipation. Try the following activities:

- Get your child to play with musical instruments such as drums, cymbals and mouth organs.

- Play an instrument and let her listen. It is great if you can play the piano, guitar or recorder well, but children are equally fascinated by the sounds made by instruments which anyone can play such as drums, whistles, mouth organs and kazoos.

- Get your child to play a musical instrument as an accompaniment to your singing or a tape. Get her to stop as soon as the music stops by asking her to put her arms in the air.

- Clap, knee bounce, hum or sway to songs to encourage a feeling for rhythm.

- Perform action rhymes to encourage listening and concentration. For example:

> Miss Polly had a dolly who was sick sick sick
> So she phoned for the doctor to come quick quick quick
> The doctor came with his bag and his hat
> And he rapped on the door with a rat-a-tat-tat.
>
> He looked at the dolly and he shook his head
> He said to Miss Polly 'Put her straight to bed'
> Then he wrote on his paper for a pill pill pill
> I'll be back in the morning yes I will will will.

- Also use some of the songs with actions listed in Chapters 3 and 4, for example 'Wind the bobbin up', page 59, 'The wheels on the bus', page 59, 'Here we go round the mulberry bush', page 59, 'I'm a little teapot', page 60, 'Ring a ring o' roses', page 99 and 'Five currant buns in the baker's shop', page 71.

- If your child has a hearing impairment, get her to touch the speakers of a CD or cassette player (make sure it won't damage them) to feel the vibrations of the music and play games using the on/off button. Put her hand on a drum or tambourine while you bang it.

- Play musical bumps, mats, chairs or statues, where your child has to listen for the music to stop and then do something: for example stand still, sit on a chair, put a hat on or jump. Use fast and slow rhythms.

- Play different types of music and encourage your child to move appropriately, for example marching, galloping and tiptoeing.

There are music and movement classes for pre-school children which use some of the ideas above. Alternatively, you could try to meet up with a few friends on a regular basis for short music sessions because it can be quite difficult to organize your own children for musical activities if you are on your own at home. Don't be embarrassed. Try singing nursery rhymes, playing musical instruments, playing some musical games and moving to music. Children love it.

CHAPTER 7

Social Development

THE THEORY

What is social development?

Social development start when a child gains an awareness that he is a separate individual, distinct from his mother and other people, and has a concept of himself and his identity. Once he has understood his own individuality he can go on to learn the skills needed to live alongside others in a community – his immediate and extended family, friends, playgroup and the wider community of neighbours. Children have to learn to mix and communicate with others, to share things and take turns, and to live by the generally accepted rules which govern each community.

Chronological development

The newborn baby

As soon as a baby is born he is a social animal. He does not want to be left alone, but finds comfort and security in being held and cuddled by other people, especially his mother. He cries to get attention and in order to have his needs met.

Interest in people

Newborn babies are programmed to find the human face the most interesting object of attention. Quite quickly, and even with the limited vision of a newborn, they study faces, either real ones or representations, and make eye contact.

Babies then usually learn to smile within weeks. Smiling has a powerful and positive impact on carers and babies get the instant reward of more attention. It is very difficult for parents to resist their baby's smile. Coos and gurgles have the same effect, binding parents closer to their baby. Babies are also learning a vital lesson. They are discovering that by smiling and making noises they can use adults to get what they need. They are also learning, at a very early stage, that people are important: this is vital because it is through other people that they will learn about themselves, about what they can do and about the world around them.

Anticipation of familiar activities

Your baby will start to become aware of familiar activities and will begin to recognize visual and sound clues which tell him what is about to happen. He learns to recognize that the sound of the bath tap running means that he is going to have a bath, or that his coat and boots appearing mean that he is going to go out. Parents recognize that their child is picking up on the 'cues of life' by signs of anticipation and excitement. Some children will start kicking and squeaking excitedly when their clothes are removed in anticipation of having a bath. It may seem obvious, but anticipating familiar situations and routines is actually a very important skill without which we would not be able to make sense of our environment. This is the basis for our own feeling of control over our lives.

Concept of self-identity

A child gradually gains a sense that he is an individual with a separate identity to his mother. He does this by learning about his own body, what it can do and how it feels. He learns that he can control his own limbs but not those of other people, that if he chews his feet he can feel it but not if he is chewing his father's fingers. At around the same time children learn that objects and people continue to exist even when they cannot be seen (object permanence, see Chapter 3, p.50). A child will scream when his mother leaves the room because as far as he is concerned she no longer exists. It is only later that he understands that she continues to exist, although she cannot be seen, and will return.

Turn-taking

Turn-taking skills are most easily observed when a parent talks to his or her child. For example, a father says something to his child who then responds with noises and then stops and waits for a response from his father before making further noises. This can continue until there has been an extended 'conversation'. Turn-taking is fundamental to communication and language skills and is therefore fully described in Chapter 4, page 88, but it is also crucial to social development since concepts of turn-taking, sharing and consideration for other people are the basis of social skills.

Getting adult attention

Newborn babies cry to get attention and then leave their parents to go through the routine of checking whether they want milk, a nappy change, sleep, winding or a cuddle. Parents soon learn to recognize different cries for hunger, pain, tiredness or boredom. Later on, children learn to use more sophisticated methods to communicate. They make different sounds and noises in different situations. These are not words but they are an important precursor to speech and demonstrate that the child is seeking to interact with other people.

An early example of this is when a child wakes up in his cot and starts shouting rather than crying to show that he is awake and wants his parents to come and get him. Another example is that when a mother is playing with her child, the child will use smiles and gurgles to keep her interest and stop her going off to do something else.

A child has to learn that he can affect, influence and manipulate people around him. He has to see the point of social interaction, in other words that he can get adults to do things which he cannot do by himself. If parents are uninterested in their child and do not respond to him appropriately, the child will lose interest in social interaction with a detrimental effect on all his development.

These early stages of interaction may lay the foundation for later behavioural problems. A child who gets lots of attention for playing nicely will, one hopes, continue in that vein, whereas a child who is ignored unless he makes a fuss may continue to use bad behaviour to gain attention in the future.

Recognition of familiar people and fear of strangers

Newborn babies recognize their parents very quickly by their smell and the sound of their voices, which will have grown familiar during pregnancy. Initially babies are not frightened of strangers and can be passed around family and friends without difficulty. However, later on they start to recognize familiar people, family, friends and relatives and, as a consequence, in self-preservation, become shy or frightened of strangers. As they gain experience and confidence that adults will not harm them, this fear of strangers diminishes.

Co-operating and copying

When children are learning early physical skills, such as sitting up, walking and placing objects, they are largely self-absorbed, experimenting by themselves. They tolerate some interventions from adults and go to an adult for needs like food and comfort.

Next, they start to co-operate with adults in play such as 'pat-a-cake' and by obeying simple commands such as 'come here' or 'give me the cup'. They help adults in play, for example with feeding a doll or rolling a ball.

At the same time they begin to copy what adults are doing, often housework activities such as wiping a table, sweeping the floor or dusting. They also start to copy gestures such as waving goodbye or saying 'sshh'. Children learn to fit into society by copying the manners and behaviours of those around them.

Sharing and turn-taking

As children understand object permanence (see Chapter 3, p.50), and as they have a concept of themselves as separate individuals, they become possessive about their belongings and toys and are reluctant to give them up to another person or child or to leave them. Equally, they have no concept of sharing the attention of an adult, for example wanting books read exclusively for them and not for their siblings or friends. Gradually the ability to share possessions and take turns in activities comes as they see that they themselves will ultimately benefit. They realize that if they give up their toys to other children now they will get them back later and others will be expected to do the same for them.

Testing the boundaries

When children learn enough self-awareness, they start to have their own desires which don't always coincide with those of their parents. Initially they can easily be distracted with a different activity. For instance, if a child wants a particular toy which someone else is using he may get cross, but will easily be placated with another equally interesting toy.

Later on, children become more determined and not so easily distracted so they may start having tantrums if thwarted. They need to know what the rules are and what the boundaries of acceptable behaviour are. They like to test the boundaries to see if they can be moved. Once they discover the limits cannot be moved they feel safe and settle down to operate within the acceptable boundaries. If they learn what these rules are, they come out of the period of tantrums much more amenable and affectionate individuals. If parents do not lay down the rules and interpret them consistently, it takes longer for their children to learn how to behave. By testing rules and boundaries children are trying to learn about the world about them.

Social interaction

Children learn to enjoy helping adults in daily tasks such as cooking, shopping and gardening, and get pleasure and fulfilment from co-operating and achieving things with adults.

Children also set up their own social networks. They want to be with other children and have friends. First of all children play with anyone who is doing what they are doing but later they start making real friends.

Understanding the feelings of others

Children sense the feelings of others, whether they are upset, sad, happy or angry. As they get older they are able to show that they understand the feelings of their friends by showing sympathy or concern, say if they hurt themselves or if they are made unhappy by an event. Children need to temper their own natural egocentricity with an interest in others and an empathy with their situation and concerns. If a child retains his egocentric view of the world into adulthood he will find it very difficult to make friends or interact socially because other people will not tolerate it for long.

Playing alone

Though social interaction is important, children need to balance it with time spent alone because this is important for relaxation and for experimentation. As adults we spend time alone to experiment and rehearse what we are going to say or how we are going to behave before we feel confident to do so publicly. Children spend short periods playing alone initially but will gradually extend their solitary play and want to go off to their own space to play for longer periods.

Learning social rules

Children learn to copy adults and to want to co-operate with them and win their approval. As their social circle extends and they make their own friends, and as they discover what is permissible behaviour and what is not, they learn to obey the social rules more generally and fit in with other people.

Parallel development

Personalities

Children are born with their own personalities – some are shy and introverted and others are extrovert and gregarious. Children's personalities should always be respected and allowed to develop with understanding.

Social play

To begin with, children play on their own but, over time, they learn to play with others in a co-operative way. This process is very gradual, so though usually differentiated in the following way it may not be easy to 'classify' a child at any one time. Genuine co-operative play is the goal, but we probably all know some 'normal' adults who aren't very good at it!

Solitary play

A child plays on his own, for example posting shapes, pushing cars or doing puzzles.

Parallel play

A child plays alongside another child but with no interaction between them. For instance, two children play in a sand pit digging and pouring sand. Both are doing the same thing but not together.

Observing play

A child becomes aware of what others are doing and is interested in it but does not actually join in. If a child goes into a playgroup and sees some children playing with Duplo, he will stop and watch them from the edge but not take the plunge and join in. Although this is identified as a separate phase, children do observe others at earlier phases of their development too.

Joining in

Children play together doing the same activity but on their own terms so although they may dress up together or help each other play with Duplo they will often end up being aggressive towards each other.

Co-operative play

This is genuinely co-operative play where children have negotiated a way of sharing an activity with each other and are able to resolve most disagreements and differences themselves. They are prepared to wait, take turns and share. For instance, they may play hide and seek with each other or Snap cards. This is highly developed play.

Imaginative play

Imaginative play is one of the ways in which children explore social situations. They may act out situations they have witnessed or take on different roles. It is also an important vehicle for them to interact with their peers by co-operating with them to act out different scenarios. It is covered more fully in Chapter 3, pages 56–57.

GAMES AND ACTIVITIES

Interest in people

Some children with special needs are withdrawn and un-interested in people, but they need to learn that there is a point to human contact.

Play eye contact games to encourage your child to interact with adults. Many different games are listed in Chapter 4, pages 94–96. Make sure you give your child time to respond.

- Play any game which your child likes, because if he enjoys it he will see the point of interacting with you. In addition, if he wants to play the game again, he will have to find a way of communicating that desire. When you play try to incorporate lots of eye contact and physical contact.

• While looking in the mirror with your child, make exaggerated and interesting faces, silly expressions and funny noises, and play peek-a-boo games. Any games with mirrors will make a child look at his own and other faces.

Make eye contact

• Dress up in silly clothes, such as hats, earrings, glasses and false noses to gain attention.

• Play with sound-making toys near your face to draw attention to yourself.

• Use face paints to make your face more interesting.

• Also use the ideas listed in the section on getting a response in Chapter 8, pages 186–189.

Anticipation of familiar activities

In daily life try to establish good routines to give your child a better chance of understanding what is happening and antici-pating what is about to happen. Try to give clues as to what is going to happen – for example, the sound of running taps for a bath, a plate and spoon before meal times, a certain location for nappy changes and so on.

Try to keep certain toys in a particular room so that your child can learn where things are kept.

Use the same language to describe things each day. Don't vary it too much because it makes it more difficult to understand.

Concept of self-identity

Play games which give your child an awareness of his body and himself. Ideas for games are described in Chapter 8, pages 189–192.

Turn-taking

Ideas for games to aid anticipation and turn-taking are listed in Chapter 4, pages 97–98.

Getting adult attention

Before being able to talk your child can request your attention in a number of ways, for example by eye-pointing, finger or hand pointing, offering a toy, tugging at you or your clothes, using natural gesture, taking your hand to an object, leading you to something or vocalizing. All methods are really helpful to you and him and show his desire for communication and social interaction.

Taking an adult by the hand

Respond to him immediately, acknowledge his request and give an immediate response whether it is a yes or a no. If he doesn't get a response from you, he might stop asking and become more withdrawn. If your child tries to interact in any way:

- Respond immediately and if possible give him what he wants since it will encourage him to try again.

- Be exaggerated in your response so he gets a big reward, either by being excessive yourself, with lots of noise and facial expressions, or, if you have a large family or a group of friends round, get them to join in the response.

It can be difficult to be sure that your child is actually trying to communicate by eye-pointing or a slight gesture but it is better to give him the benefit of the doubt. Even if he isn't it might encourage him to try and won't do any harm. If you take a negative view you may be ignoring his efforts.

Early communication skills are described more fully in Chapter 4, pages 87–92.

Co-operating in games with an adult

- Get your child to give you objects and toys. Hold out your hand and ask for whatever he has in his hands at the time and see if he will release it into your hands.

- Roll a ball or car between you and your child.

- Play 'Round and round the garden' and get him to hold out his hand in readiness for you (see p.99 for words).

- Try any singing games where your child has to co-operate with you with his movements. You might:

  - Hold your child's hands in yours and get him to clap, singing 'pat-a-cake' (see p.59), or other clapping songs.

  - Sing 'My hands and your hands' over and over again while alternately clapping your own hands together and then clapping your child's.

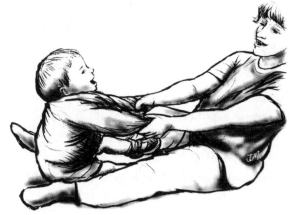

'Row, row, row your boat...'

- Sing 'Row, row, row your boat' or 'See-saw Margery Daw' (the words are on p.96). Hold your child's hands and pretend to row so that he has to co-operate with your movements.

- Similarly, you can use 'Have you ever ever ever in your long legged life' (see p.96 for words). Lay your child on his back and, holding his ankles, move his legs round and round with bent knees in a cycling motion.

- Hold your child on your knee, facing you and with the palms of your hands together sway to:

> My bonny lies over the ocean
> My bonny lies over the sea
> My bonny lies over the ocean
> Oh bring back my bonny to me
> Bring back, bring back
> Oh bring back my bonny to me, to me
> Bring back, bring back
> Oh bring back my bonny to me.

- Use any rhyme with a beat to sway or row together. Or hold your child in your arms and hum, swaying to the music.

- Play tug of war games. For example, use a rope with hoops on it which he can see moving from one end to the other as each of you pulls the rope in turn.

- Use opportunities as they arise for 'to and fro' games. For instance, if your child pulls you back by a rucksack strap or a shirt tail, move forwards and wait for him to pull you back. These situations just arise naturally and although they can seem irritating are actually very useful opportunities for interaction.

Copying an adult

In social situations show your child what to do and what is expected of him. But don't expect him to co-operate for long. If you want him to sit down to drink his milk, sit down yourself and drink your coffee. Set a good example in all things!

Other ideas for copying are included in Chapter 3, pages 58–60 and Chapter 4, page 100.

Sharing and turn-taking

As children start interacting with others, they have to develop an ability to share and take turns. You have to insist that your child obeys the rules and does not snatch toys away from others but allows them to use his toys and belongings. You also have to ensure that others do the same for him so that he can see the benefits of obeying the rules. Make sure, therefore, that you are fair and even-handed and that other adults do the same for your child.

- Have a teddy bear's picnic and get your child to share food fairly between the participants.

- If you go out to feed the ducks make a conscious effort to give some to one duck and then some to another and some more to another and so on.

- Share out food at meal times – some for John, some for Jane, some for Mummy and some for Daddy. Share out things like raisins or sweets like Smarties and chocolate buttons.

- Get your child to play turn-taking games with his peers such as siblings or friends at home or in playgroups. This will give him an opportunity to learn to obey simple social rules. Playgroups and playgrounds can be very good for this because children have to wait their turns to use equipment like trampolines, slides or swings and to learn to give things up for others. Again, make sure your child is getting a fair deal.

Testing the boundaries

Techniques for behaviour management are covered in detail in Chapter 9, pages 195–203.

Social interaction

Get your child to help you in everyday activities like tucking in sheets, using a dustpan and brush, polishing furniture, cooking, pushing a pushchair jointly, or carrying a basket or bag jointly.

Understanding the feelings of others

Take every opportunity to talk about emotions as they come up in daily life or in books and videos.

For other ideas for activities see also Chapter 8, page 194.

Playing alone

Select a toy or game which your child enjoys and can play without adult help. Sit in the same room and talk him through the game but do not get physically involved. Aim for only a few minutes to begin with. Gradually say less and extend the time period.

Playing alone

Find an interesting book or photograph album and encourage your child to look at it by himself but stay nearby.

Learning social rules

Children take time to learn what is acceptable behaviour in different circumstances and situations.

Avoid social situations which your child cannot handle if this is at all possible. There is no point putting you and him through stressful situations if they are not necessary. For example, you don't have to take your child to a posh restaurant when a pizza place would do. When your child's behaviour has improved you can try again.

There are some situations which are unavoidable, like hospital visits and shoe shopping. When you are faced with these try the following ideas:

- Talk your child through every situation very simply, involve him in what is going on and give him something to concentrate on. If you are going round the supermarket, talk about what you are buying, what colour it is, its size and qualities and anticipate what you are going to buy next.

People may think you are slightly odd but that is better than having an hysterical child.

- Give your child something to do in a situation which is likely to throw him. If your child always misbehaves in certain shops give him a special toy as you go in, as this may distract him for a while.

- If you are going shopping, give your child his own shopping list made with pictures or labels so he can get some things by himself.

- If, for example, you are going on a holiday or your child is going into hospital, prepare him for the new experience by talking about what is going to happen and by showing him relevant pictures, photographs or books.

- If you are having problems with specific situations, start off by practising at home, then introduce other people into the exercise before taking your child out to a friend's house and finally into a normal situation. For example, you might be having problems getting your child to sit still to eat meals in strange environments because he finds it too interesting or disturbing. So going to birthday parties or out for meals is very difficult. Start by being rigid at home about sitting down to eat or drink. When friends come round insist on the same behaviour. When you go to a friend's house do the same and when you have the behaviour established, attempt a bigger gathering – a birthday party, playgroup tea or restaurant meal. Build up the time spent sitting at the table.

Ultimately it is repeated experience of a situation which makes a child understand what he is or is not supposed to do. In the end there may be nothing else you can do but persevere using the behaviour management techniques to reinforce good behaviour. See Chapter 9, pages 196–197 .

When my son first had to wear glasses he used to go berserk in the opticians – trying on all the glasses, pulling the contact lens solutions off the shelf, trying to play with the till etc. despite the fact that it had a lovely play area for children. After six months of constant visits (because he was forever breaking his glasses), he has learnt to behave better and will head for the play area straightaway.

Gender issues

Don't stereotype your child. Give him the opportunity to play with toys of all kinds and to do all sorts of activities regardless of gender. Allow and encourage boys to play with dolls and to cook, and allow and encourage girls to play with train sets and cars.

Developing social play

Before you start on social play make sure the fundamentals of eye contact, turn-taking and co-operation are well established.

Parallel play (playing alongside another child)

Children first play with an adult because adults are more predictable and controllable than other children, so the first step towards getting your child to play alongside another is to get him to play alongside you. Copy what he does, so if he crawls, you crawl; if he builds a tower with bricks you do the same.

Respect a child's sense of personal space. The amount of personal space we need is affected by cultural factors and some children with special needs, such as autistic children, also need greater space than others.

Get your child to participate in a singing session at a playgroup or mother and toddler group – these will require him to play alongside another child in a non-threatening away.

Go to playgrounds and encourage your child to play on the slides, swings, and climbing frames because they are a good starting point for a child to play alongside other children.

Encourage your child to do some constructive play that he enjoys while another child is doing the same thing; for example Duplo, painting, drawing, sand and water play. Contrary to what might be expected, children co-operate better in a controlled environment than during free time. If your child has siblings of a suitable age then they would be the obvious first playmates because they are familiar and you will find plenty of opport-unities to share games. Alternatively, you could set up play with children whom he sees regularly at home or at playgroup.

Joining in play (playing with another child)

Once your child is playing alongside other children happily, it is likely that interaction will come automatically.

Try simple and easy games such as peek-a-boo games or turn-taking games (putting marbles in a marble run, running cars down a shoot). It's also good to try a game where there are two interdependent actions. One child might do one element and the other child complete it. For example, one child puts an object in and the other presses a switch for it to fall out.

When your child with special needs joins in with his peers, you may have to consider how he is treated. Children with special needs are often in danger of either being 'mothered' by other children or being bullied and teased. It is up to the playgroup and parents to set the tone and to give children the understanding to treat children with special needs with compassion but also with respect. Don't be afraid to point things out to others, they're probably oblivious to the problem.

CHAPTER 8

Emotional Development

THE THEORY

What is emotional development?

Emotional development in the early years involves a child's gaining an awareness of herself. She learns that she is a separate individual, that she has a body and a name, and that she can influence and affect her environment and the people around her. Her personality and her early upbringing jointly lay the foundations for how she will feel about herself later in life, her self-esteem, confidence and behaviour. Later she will learn that she and other people have different emotions at different times and how to deal with them.

Chronological development

The newborn baby

Newborn babies seek human contact and comfort. Initially they can only cry to show that they want attention and company. But they soon learn to smile and vocalize and, if parents respond quickly and appropriately, discover that this behaviour is more useful for getting attention and entertainment.[1]

Love

All children need love and security. They need adults who are responsive to them. Children need to be in a loving and secure

---

[1] See Holmes, J. (1993) *John Bowlby and Attachment Theory.* London: Routledge.

181

Children need love

environment where they feel safe and valued and therefore have the confidence to take risks, make mistakes and learn from them.

Children who are not secure may become withdrawn or timid or, more likely, become badly behaved or even aggressive in an effort to gain adult attention. These children will need more love and should be given attention for the positive things that they do rather than for their transgressions (see Chapter 9, pp.196–197). Children need sufficient stimulation, then time to think and respond; they do not need over-stimulation.

Children, however, should not be overprotected and smothered in love. They need to have the space to gain independence from their family.

Responding to physical contact

After they have learnt to smile, children start to enjoy more active physical contact like cuddles, tickles and gentle physical play. They show their enjoyment by smiling, vocalizing, and later chuckling and laughing.

Physical self-awareness

A baby initially has no real concept of herself as a physical and separate person. She may just see herself as an extension of her mother's body. She will gradually learn that she has her own body and where it begins and ends.

Children start to explore what their hands can do by passing them in front of their face, playing with their fingers and working out that they can control them. Similarly, they bring their feet up and investigate them by putting them in their mouth. As children develop physically and are able to sit up, crawl and walk, they learn more about themselves and their bodies.

These experiments give children an understanding of what and where their bodies are and how they can control them. They underlie emotional development since a child needs an understanding of her physical body before she can have any notion of her mind and emotions.

Concept of self

Children gain an awareness of themselves as individuals with their own minds. They play peek-a-boo games and become aware that things continue to exist even when they cannot be seen. They start to recognize and respond to their own names.

Dependence on a familiar adult

Children initially like adult company but are not heavily dependent on their mother or principal carer. They can be passed from one adult to another and later play contentedly by themselves. As they become more aware of things going on around them, they become more anxious and will tend to cling to their mother if she tries to leave them. As children gain greater confidence and a sense of security they will once again tolerate being left.

Sharing

As children gain an understanding of who they are, they also become aware of what belongs to them, and can be quite possessive about their toys, their parents and their environment. It takes time before they develop an ability to share things with other children and to take turns.

Recognizing themselves

When children first see themselves in a mirror, they think their reflection is another person and try to touch it and interact with it. However eventually they recognize themselves in the mirror and in photographs.

They also soon start acquiring an idea of their body image – whether they are a boy or a girl, whether they are tall or short, and so on. They detect differences between other people and themselves very early on so it is important that their self-esteem is built up from an early age.

Self-esteem

Children need to develop their self-esteem in order to gain the confidence to leave the family environment and take risks in their social, educational and work life. Children who have high self-esteem tend to feel more fulfilled and happier as adults than those who do not.

Parents are the first and most important people to contribute towards generating self-esteem. By praising their child for things she has done rather than telling her off for things she has not, by valuing her achievements – whether they are attempts to talk or pictures exhibited on the fridge – and by giving her the trust, freedom, space and opportunity to venture out and try new experiences and opportunities, parents contribute to their child's perception of her abilities and their value.

Choices are also important in a child's life. A child who is never given any choice in what she does may become passive or confrontational. Being able to make choices is an important skill in itself; but it is also one of the things that makes our lives worth living. It gives us our sense of control, independence and autonomy.

Children therefore need to make choices in their lives. At a simple level it may be the choice between an apple and banana for pudding or different books or toys to play with. Later, when they have the understanding, children can be asked to make more complex choices such as whether they want to go swimming or to the park.

Children also need to learn to be able to cope with not succeeding and to develop ways of accepting their failures, putting them in perspective, learning from them and trying again. Children pick up their parents' attitudes to failure by seeing how they respond. If a child is having difficulty getting dressed, she could either throw her clothes down in frustration or try again perhaps seeking parental help. She may make this decision based on seeing how her own parents react to things going wrong.

Sense of security

Parents set boundaries for what is acceptable behaviour for their children. Children test those boundaries and ideally find that they are consistent and immovable. Children then know what is expected of them. They also feel that their parents are in control not only of their own family but also of the wider world too. This gives children a sense of security and safety which helps their emotional development. This does not mean, however, that children cannot have choices within those boundaries.

If the boundaries are always shifting, children don't know what is expected of them and they will feel insecure. In addition, children will see that their parents can be controlled by them, in which case their parents can't possibly be in control of their own family circle – let alone the world beyond.

Fears

At some point, most children are afraid of falling or of strangers. Later they can develop other fears. Some are rational like a fear of dogs if they have been bitten; some are acquired from other people, like a fear of spiders acquired from a parent; and others are irrational, like a fear of monsters or falling down the toilet. These last fears often come as their imagination develops ahead of their understanding of language and the world about them or from simple misunderstandings. For example, a small child became frightened of going to bed at night. It transpired that she was frightened by 'draughts'. She had no understanding of what a draught was, but her mother said each night, 'I'll tuck you up nice and tight to keep the draughts out' and so she was terrified!

Understanding and expressing emotions

Children grow to recognize emotions in other people like anger, happiness, pain and surprise. They later learn to respond appropriately by seeking to comfort others who have hurt themselves or expressing happiness at another child's birthday. Children learn to express emotions such as affection for brothers and sisters. They also learn which emotions it is not socially acceptable to express. For example, for many people in our culture boys aren't supposed to cry and girls shouldn't express open aggression. It is debatable whether this is a good thing or not.

Whether children grow up to be assertive and able to say 'no' to other people, to be passive and heavily influenced by others or to be aggressive and bully others, is influenced by their parents and by their innate personality.

Growing independence

Children gradually gain independence from their parents. They get to a stage when they want to do everything by themselves but they can't because it's not safe or they don't have the physical capability. This often leads to temper tantrums because they don't understand why their activities are being curtailed. However, as they develop their skills and their understanding, they may safely do more by themselves.

Space to gain independence

GAMES AND ACTIVITIES

Getting a response

Some children with special needs are unresponsive and uninterested in people and their environment. This is one of the hardest things for parents to cope with. Parents usually strive both subconsciously and consciously to find things that will elicit

a response from their child and it is vitally important that parents of unresponsive and passive children do not reject their child but continue to show them affection by smiling, talking and cuddling them and by seeking activities which they may enjoy.

> Before we even knew our son had problems we had found instinctively that the one thing that seemed to elicit a response was tickling games and we used to play them a lot. The first time he ever initiated play with us was when, at about 18 months, he held out his hand by himself as a request for more 'Round and round the garden'. It was a wonderful moment.

Often you may find yourself wondering if what gives pleasure to your child is of any use to her, whether it is tickling, bubbles or rough play. It is. To see your child enjoying herself is not only wonderful in itself for you but it is also a spur and a stimulation to all sorts of other activities for her. A child who likes bubbles may learn to point to or say 'bubbles', or to crawl to the bubbles, or to play at bubbles with other children.

You will know when your child is responding to something that is going on, even if the response is very slight. Build on it.

Below are some ideas for activities which might appeal to your child. Remember that children with special needs often take longer to respond so give your child plenty of time.

Don't reject an unresponsive child

Get your child's attention

First of all get your child's attention by doing something out of the ordinary which will alert her to the fact that something unusual is about to happen. A visual prompt like putting on an extravagant hat is probably the easiest. You could also use some of the ideas for gaining eye contact listed in Chapter 4, pages 94–96.

Visually exciting toys

There are all sorts of things which might interest your child, for example very brightly coloured toys – and particularly those with flashing lights – also lights like torches, disco lights or fibre-optic lights. Children often love wind-up mechanical toys, friction cars and bubbles.

Physical play

- Play tickling games including 'Round and round the garden' and 'This little piggy'. For the words see Chapter 4, page 99.

- Do knee rides like 'Horsey, horsey don't you stop' and 'Humpty Dumpty'. For words and more examples see Chapter 4, page 99.

- Cuddle her.

- Do some rough play, for example rolling your child around the bed, throwing her in the air and catching her, swirling her round and round in your arms, bouncing up and down holding her.

Sound

Use musical activities:

- Play any musical instrument whether it is the guitar, recorder, kazoo or drum.

- Sing nursery rhymes or your favourite pop song to your child.

- Play with musical toys like keyboards or musical spinning tops.

- Take your child to listen to live music – perhaps buskers in the street.

One day we were looking round Winchester Cathedral and happened to coincide with a rehearsal by the Bournemouth Symphony Orchestra. Our son was stunned by the sound of the full orchestra with the beautiful acoustics and we couldn't get him away.

Smell

- Try making 'smelly boxes'. Put aromatic substances like spices, coffee grains, tea or orange in a small box like a Tic-Tac box for your child to smell.

- Dab some perfume, aftershave, Dettol etc. on a ball of cotton wool and let your child smell it.

- Use aromatherapy oils.

Touch

- Find different textures on household objects to give your child different sensations – smooth (silk and velvet), rough, spiky (brush), lumpy, cold, warm, hard (stone), soft (fur), etc.

Physical self-awareness

- Stroke, touch and massage parts of your child's body.

- Play with her hands and feet by holding and shaking them.

- Play gentle tickling games, for example, running your finger up the length of her body.

- Place your child in a confined space or near to a wall so that when she moves she makes contact with another surface.

- Give your child rattles, because when she moves her hand, she will have the movement reinforced by the sound. As well as hand-held rattles, you can use wrist rattles or mittens with bells sewn into them. Even if your child cannot grasp things she can still learn about her body. Similarly, you can attach bells or small rattles to socks to encourage kicking.

Concept of self

The first body parts that a child learns to recognize are usually eyes, nose and mouth followed by hair, tummy and hands.

- Use opportunities as they come up naturally to name different body parts. Bath-time is the most obvious time as you wash each part, but you can also use nappy changing to name tummy, bottom, legs etc. and getting dressed to talk about arms, hands, feet etc.

- Sing songs such as 'Pat-a-cake', see page 59 for the words, or:

Head and shoulders, knees and toes, knees and toes
Head and shoulders, knees and toes, knees and toes
And eyes and ears and mouth and nose
Head, shoulders, knees and toes, knees and toes.

Tommy thumb, Tommy thumb, where are you?
Here I am, here I am and how do you do?

> *Other verses:*
> Peter pointer, Peter pointer, where are you?…
> Middle man, middle man, where are you?…
> Ruby ring, ruby ring, where are you?…
> Baby small, baby small, where are you?…

- Draw or use big clear pictures of faces and name the body parts.
- Sit your child on your knee and touch different parts of her body and your own as you name them, for example 'My knee. Your knee'.
- Use dolls to name body parts.
- Use mirrors to make your child look at herself while playing the following games:
  - Get her to touch different parts of her face.
  - Repeat her name as you point to her reflection.
  - Try putting a smudge of lipstick or shaving foam on her nose or cheeks. Either wipe it off yourself or get her to do it, so that she can appreciate that she is looking at herself.
  - Using a big mirror, make lots of silly faces and noises and see if you can encourage her to copy.
  - Play peek-a-boo games with the mirror, hiding the mirror then showing your child her face.

Awareness of name

This requires a lot of repetition and perseverance. Name your child at every opportunity. Ask 'Where's Sophie? There's Sophie' while touching her chest with your finger and giving a big smile.

Ask questions like 'Who has got the ball? Jonathan's got the ball'.

Parents naturally talk to their child in the third person – 'It's Emma's cup' rather than 'It's your cup'. This is good because it reinforces identity.

Sharing

- Play games where your child has to divide things between people and toys; for instance, a tea party for dolls or teddies where the food has to be given to each doll or teddy.

- Get your child to hand out food to other people as well as herself, for instance a biscuit for you and for her.

- Get your child to share some food or a toy with you or one other familiar person and get other children to do the same with her.

Recognizing self in mirror and photographs

Use the mirror games described in the section on awareness of self (above) to encourage your child to see her own image and recognize it by pointing at it.

Use a mirror

Create a photograph album or a box of pictures of your family which your child can look at. It is good to use spare not-so-great photographs for this which you don't mind being damaged. Look through the album with your child naming the family members in each picture. Ask your child to find pictures of different people and of herself.

Building up self-esteem

When a child has special needs and is aware of the difference between herself and other children, particularly perhaps because she has a physical disability or a sensory impairment, she needs even more support and encouragement to give her confidence and self-esteem.

Praise your child for her achievements. Children need masses of praise for things that they do and things that they try to do. Even if they do not always succeed, parents need to show appreciation for the effort shown. Children thrive on praise. They love the attention and will strive to repeat what they have done. It is a powerful motivator.

Show your appreciation of any work that your child has done. The fridge is a good place for a rotating exhibition but it is also good to have a noticeboard on which you can pin things or to display models and paintings round the room. Ask your child, 'Who painted the picture? Yes, Mary did. It's beautiful'. Show them to family and friends and get them to join in the praise.

Use songs to increase self-esteem and confidence. Children generally find them enjoyable and fun and it's a non-threatening way of getting a child to do something which she cannot fail at. Songs with actions are particularly good because a child can join in with as little or as much as she can achieve and it does not matter if she cannot do it all. There are many examples in Chapter 3, pages 70–71 and Chapter 4, page 99. If you sing 'Wind the bobbin up', for example, and your child does the clapping, you can praise that. Your child feels she has achieved something and everyone has enjoyed themselves. As the child's confidence and abilities grow, she will be able to do more.

Sing nursery rhymes and substitute your child's name in the song. For example sing 'Baa, baa black sheep' and instead of saying 'little boy who lives down the lane' sing 'little Ben who lives down the lane' or 'little Anna who lives down the lane'. Also try 'Rock-a-bye baby' singing 'Rock-a-bye Lauren on a tree top' or 'Rock-a-bye Nick Nick on a tree top'.

Encourage your child to play with water and sand because there is no right or wrong way to play – it is about exploring and experimenting.

Give your child good examples of how to cope with failure by your response to her failure and to your own. Show her that it is all right to fail and not to be very good at something and that it is the effort and the drive to try again that is valued.

Be positive in your approach as described in Chapter 2, pages 39–41.

Remember not to make praise valueless by overdoing it. If a skill is fairly well established you do not need to go overboard. Equally, if your child has not really made much of an effort then don't collude with her by praising her work. You will have to be sensitive to your child. If it is an achievement for your child to sit still and do any painting at all, praise her. If, on the other hand, your child is capable of sustained effort, don't praise a few marks on a piece of paper excessively.

Also see the section 'Caring Start' in Chapter 3, pages 84–86.

Making a choice

It is important to find ways of offering choices to children with special needs and of enabling them to communicate their choice.

If you give your child a choice, she must be able to understand what you are asking and be able to show in some way what she wants by eye-pointing, pointing, signing or speaking. To begin with, you may actually need to have the objects in front of you so

Use pictures to give your child a choice of activities

that she can clearly understand and select. To offer her a choice of fruit for tea, show her an apple and a banana and ask her which she would like. If she chooses an apple, by eye pointing or pointing, hide the banana and say 'You want the apple' and give it to her.

Easy choices are of food, drinks and games where you can show the choice. For more complex choices you may have to show some wellies to indicate going out or photographs or pictures of activities such as swimming or going to the park.

Caring Start, which is described in Chapter 3, pages 84–86, is an approach which aims to give children choices in their lives.

Understanding feelings

- Show pictures of people expressing emotions and talk about them in simple language.
- Read books which show people expressing emotions.
- Explain what is happening around your child. 'He's hurt his knee. He's unhappy.' 'It's her birthday. She's happy.'
- If your child does something which affects someone else emotionally, explain it: 'You knocked him over. He's crying. Poor Oscar.'
- Use a mirror to show a happy face, a sad face, a surprised face, an angry face etc.
- Express emotions yourself and talk about them.
- Play imaginatively with your child, using different scenarios to show emotions such as dolly unwell or dolly falling over.

CHAPTER 9

Additional Practical Advice

BEHAVIOUR

Deciding what is and isn't appropriate behaviour for your child is difficult enough at the best of times. With a child with special needs it can be tricky to establish the right balance between making allowances for a child's lack of understanding, on the one hand, and being overly strict in order to get her to conform and fit in, on the other.

How to change bad behaviour
Look at what the behaviour means

Bad behaviour is a form of communication in any child. For a child with communication problems it may be one of the few ways to communicate and probably the most effective. If your child is behaving badly see what she is 'saying' to you.

If your child is often badly behaved, look at what is happening in terms of the ABC of behaviour:

- A = *Antecedents*. Look at what led up to the bad behaviour.

- B = *Behaviour*. Look at the bad behaviour and what your response is.

- C = *Consequences*. Look at what your child gets out of the incident.

Example

A child might be playing nicely but then starts attacking her baby sister, so you tell her off and distract her with a new activity.

- *Antecedents* = She has been playing for some time and has become bored or fed up. Your attention is largely going to her little sister.

- *Behaviour* = She behaves badly by yanking her sister's hair, you get very angry and shout at her, so she gets lots of attention from you.

- *Consequences* = She gets a change of activity which she wanted.

In other situations bad behaviour might mean 'I don't know how to handle this situation', 'I want some attention', 'This is too difficult', 'I can't bear this loud noise', 'I want to do something different' or 'I am tired.'

Say 'no' quietly but firmly

When your child does something unacceptable like hit another child or pinch biscuits, say 'no' quietly and firmly with a hand movement to reinforce it. Do not make a fuss, do not get angry and upset. She will then understand that her behaviour is unacceptable but she does not see you wound up and annoyed.

Then try to distract her by showing her a different toy or activity or by offering her an alternative. For example, if your child pulls someone's hair, say 'no' and then suggest that she stroke the other child's hair instead – it is difficult to stroke and pull at the same time.

Reward good behaviour and ignore bad behaviour

The golden rule of behaviour management is to reward good behaviour and ignore bad behaviour. You might think that in order to encourage good behaviour you should come down heavily on your child and 'discipline' bad behaviour. But it doesn't work. **The key is to ignore bad behaviour.** If you make a big fuss of bad behaviour, your child will get exactly what she wants, which is attention, and will have every incentive to carry on. If, on the other hand, you ignore bad behaviour, your child will achieve nothing. But at the same time you must give her attention when she behaves well.

Parents should therefore give lots of attention to their child when she is behaving well by talking to her, praising her and acknowledging her good behaviour. On the other hand, if a child behaves badly she should be given as little attention as possible or, even better, ignored (provided it is safe) so that she learns that bad behaviour is not the way to get parental attention.

It is worth remembering that we often praise children when they do something new and wonderful, get angry when they do something naughty, but ignore them when they are just doing what they are supposed to do, although this is, in fact, good behaviour. Try to praise and reward your child for just playing nicely.

If your child throws a tantrum, ignore it. Don't remonstrate or reason with your child just ignore her and wait for her to emerge from her tantrum. Never let it succeed, otherwise your child will learn that it is a good way to get what she wants and she will throw a tantrum every time she is thwarted.

Look for patterns of bad behaviour

If you examine the ABC of behaviour and can see a pattern emerging from the bad behaviour, try to pre-empt the situation before it occurs. If, for example, your child behaves badly when she gets bored, make sure you give her attention earlier by joining in her play or introducing some change.

Some situations which trigger bad behaviour are unavoidable so you have to develop a strategy for dealing with them. These are often when you cannot give attention or when a child does not understand what is happening. Find something to distract or occupy your child when the inevitable happens. For example, if your child is naughty when you are talking on the phone, have a box of special toys which you keep by the phone and give to her when the phone rings. See the section on learning social rules in Chapter 7, pages 177–178, for other ideas.

You might find it helpful to keep a diary of behavioural problems to identify trigger points and times of the day when particular behaviour occurs. From this you could work out the behaviour to be tackled and in what order.

In addition

Be consistent and never give in

If you have said no you must stick to your decision and not give in because children must learn that when you say 'no' you mean 'no'. If a child knows that you will give in if she persists, you are going to make matters worse for yourself.

Think of the child who keeps demanding biscuits. If you have a policy of giving just one, the child soon learns and will not persist once she has had her ration. If on the other hand you sometimes give in, she knows that if she whines on sufficiently she may eventually get her extra biscuit.

A child needs to know what the boundaries of acceptable behaviour are and she cannot if they are constantly changing. Some people sit down and decide what their house rules are and others will decide as they go along. If you decide that it is okay to stand on the sofa one day then you should not change your mind the next.

If you start to use these ideas on behaviour management you may find things seem more difficult before they get better because your child will be determined to break down your resistance and find out where those boundaries are. Be strong, stay firm and persevere.

However, if you are wrong, then don't be afraid to admit it and change your mind since you must also be fair and just. Sometimes you say 'no' to your child and then discover that someone else has already given permission, in which case you can say: 'Okay, Grandpa said "yes".'

Respond immediately

You should respond immediately to bad behaviour, otherwise your child will not understand what you are talking about when you do respond.

If your child behaves badly at a party, pinching other children's food for instance, you must tell her off straightaway, not wait till you get home and say, 'You were very naughty at the party' when she will have no idea what you mean. Even if you were to say 'You were very naughty pinching little Johnny's food at the party', she may still not be able to make the connection. You must make a very direct response.

You must also remember that when you praise your child or tell her off you must tell her what she is doing that is right or wrong. Rather than say 'good girl' or 'naughty girl', you should say 'good eating' or 'no, no hair pulling'. This way you are reinforcing your message. If you just say 'good' or 'bad', she does not necessarily know what she is being praised or criticized for. For the child's self-esteem it is important that you criticize the behaviour and not the child.

Other issues in behaviour management
Modifying inappropriate behaviour

Children with special needs can often learn behaviours which need to be changed later. Sometimes they learn to do something which is fine at the time but which they then use, indiscriminately, in a manner which you think is inappropriate. An example is if a child learns to kiss but then kisses everyone from granny to the gas man.

Inappropriate behaviour: kissing the gas man

If your child has learnt a behaviour which you wish to change you will need to find an alternative action which you can show your child instead. So the child who kisses everybody could be shown how to say or sign 'hello' and the child who applauds could be shown how to say or sign 'good'.

Bouncing on furniture may be fine when your child is small but not so acceptable as she gets older. Try to change her behaviour gradually by saying she cannot bounce on the chairs only on the sofa, then later only on her bed, progressing to only on the trampoline at playgroup.

Creating the right environment

Every family has a different view of what is strict and lax and there is no right or wrong but it is worth thinking of the following points.

Parents need to set limits of what is acceptable and un-acceptable behaviour. The rules should be fair, predictable, consistent and understandable. Children will set out to find those limits and to test them to see if they can be moved. Once they have found out the rules and have seen that they are enforced consistently they will feel secure and safe. For their own sakes parents need their children to work within a known framework and also because it will make them more acceptable in society.

However, parents also need to make sure that there is enough freedom for children to explore and investigate so that they are not kept in a strait-jacket but can experiment, learn and gain independence. You have to give control to gain control.

All rules are made to be broken and children need to learn that there is flexibility in all systems. Bedtime may always be seven o'clock but if it is bonfire night an exception can be made. Explain the reasons to your child.

Parents must provide good role models. The old adage 'Do as I say not as I do' should not be followed. Children copy physical examples more than they listen to words.

On a practical level, don't make things more difficult for yourself than they have to be. If your child misbehaves with your CD collection, put it out of her reach.

Choices

Children need some choice in their lives but the choices need to be appropriate to their level of understanding. There is little point asking a child whether she wants to go to France or Spain for her holiday since she will have no understanding of what this means. However, she might be able to understand the choice between wearing her yellow or red T-shirt.

It is also counter-productive to offer a child a choice when you know that only one option is viable or when you will overrule her choice. An example might be if you ask a child if she wants to go to the swings or to the beach; she decides on the beach and you then decide you want to go to the swings anyway. If there is not a genuine choice, do not give her the choice, just tell her what is going to happen.

However, choices within a child's abilities (what she wants to eat, which toys she wants to play with) are important for a child's self-esteem, independence and life skills. It is also important that parents recognize that children have views and desires and that these should be respected. A child who is deprived of choice in her life may become passive or badly behaved.

Incentives

Star charts can help if your child has the necessary level of understanding. Decide on the behaviours you want to discourage or encourage, then draw up a chart and tell your child what she has to do. Award a star as appropriate and if she gets the right number give her a small reward.

> We tried a special mat for Douglas and whenever he became so hyped-up that he was out of control we put him on it to calm down. He soon found it so helpful that he would ask to sit on it when he recognized that he was losing control. Later it became a magical mat which took him off to exotic lands.

Self-abuse

Some children abuse themselves by head-banging, biting themselves or pulling their hair out. This can be dangerous and is very distressing for parents to witness.

If your child does abuse herself, try to find the reason why. Usually it is frustration because of her inability to make herself understood, but it can be because she is frightened or confused. Perhaps she is trying to make you understand something, but can't; then she tries again and still she can't, until she is so upset that she either attacks someone else or herself. You must try to read her message before she gets so upset and angry. So use the methods described above. Look at when such behaviour is likely to happen and avoid those situations occurring.

If you cannot prevent the situation occurring have a distraction ready for your child straightaway. Failing that, give her something else to vent her anger on like a pillow to punch, or a squeaky toy to bite.

If you cannot prevent the self-abuse occurring, intervene to stop your child from causing too much harm but try not to draw attention to it.

As your child is better able to understand what is going on and communicate her needs, the self-abuse will probably stop.

Hannah kept biting her wrists with frustration. We made arm bands from old shoulder pads and Velcro and although she still bit into them it was easier to ignore as there was no blood! Eventually she stopped biting.

Other points to remember

If your child likes doing things which are extremely irritating but not dangerous, find a time and a situation when she can legitimately play. If she likes bouncing on furniture, borrow a trampoline or go to a gym class. If she likes playing with taps and water, make it a play activity each day. If your child has a lot of energy which can turn to aggression, give her opportunities to use up her energy by physical play (in the park, playground or soft play session). This is particularly important if your child has obsessions. Allow her to pursue the ones which are safe and acceptable to you and only stop those which are dangerous and anti-social. You cannot stop a child having obsessions, so if you stop one she will only find another. Children with autism will feel more secure if they have time to indulge their obsessions. If they are denied they become anxious and seek to indulge them all the time, because they never know when the next opportunity will arise.

Children need to learn that whereas some behaviour is appropriate at home it may not be elsewhere, and that situations do vary. You must explain to your child that although it is acceptable to jump on the bed at home, it is not acceptable at Granny's house and you must insist that she stops. Similarly, your child may enjoy throwing stones into a river, which is fine if no-one is around but dangerous when people are paddling nearby.

Try to remain positive even if faced with behavioural problems. For every negative thing you say make sure you find at least one positive thing to say to your child. Ensure that you begin and end each day on a positive note. Remember that if you say 'no' all the time your child will learn to ignore you. An emphatic 'no' has a lot of impact if it comes rarely but will have no effect at all if it has been said dozens of times.

Remember that your child may have a problem with sensory integration and her bad behaviour may be because she cannot bear the information that her senses are giving her, such as the feel or texture of things, noises, visual stimulation, motion etc. See if there is a pattern and, if so, seek advice.

Strategies for parents to cope with their child's poor behaviour

Family, friends and other people, who are not aware of how your child's problems affect her behaviour, may misjudge her as 'naughty' or 'badly brought-up'. Parents have then the double stress of dealing with both the behaviour and people's reactions to it. In addition, everybody has different priorities and different standards. People find it is easy to see where a child fails to come up to their own standards but they rarely notice when her behaviour exceeds them. Don't worry about other people's views. Just work on your own priorities.

For your own sanity, concentrate on two or three major problems at any one time, for instance pulling hair and running off in the car park. It is impossible to tackle all behaviour issues at once.

Make sure all the people who care for your child – grandparents, playgroups and childminders – follow the same approach with your child so that she has total consistency.

If your child has behavioural problems it can be very stressful. Try to find activities which your child enjoys and for which she behaves well, like going swimming or to the swings, and make sure you do them quite frequently so you have some positive times together.

Find activities which your child enjoys

SLEEP

If you are happy with your child's sleeping (or non-sleeping) habits then carry on and ignore other people's comments. They are only a problem if you think they are a problem. If, however, you do decide that you are fed up with your child staying up late, having disturbed nights, waking early in the mornings or with finding your child in your bed with you, then you are being perfectly reasonable to want to change things. It is within everyone's rights to expect a decent night's sleep. This is true for you and your child.

Parents need some time in the evening for their own activities as well as a good night's rest. It is much easier to cope if you know that at seven or eight o'clock your child will go to bed and stay there until a reasonable time in the morning. For your child, learning to go to sleep on her own and to sleep through the night is a vital life skill. We all feel much better after a good night's sleep.

If you are going to tackle sleep habits you must be ready and determined. **The most important rule is that once you have started you must not stop** because if you do you will send completely the wrong message to your child, i.e. that she can control you rather than that you control her, and next time you attempt to control her sleep patterns it will be even more difficult.

If you decide to change your child's sleeping habits you will probably find things get worse before they get better. You will probably get less sleep in the short term and at night, when you are tired, you will have to cope emotionally and physically with seeing your child unhappy and distressed. It is probably best to leave sleep training until you are so fed up that you are determined to sort it out once and for all. However, if there is any reason why it might be particularly difficult to leave a child to cry – for example, you or another child is unwell or you have friends staying whom you don't want disturbed – it will weaken your resolve. Put sleep training off until you are ready.

- Make sure your partner and other members of the family are in support; follow your plan and if possible share the burden so that you can get some sleep.

- Be prepared for it to take some time but be confident that all habits can be changed if you are strong enough and consistent enough.

The theory of sleep training

Children need to learn to go to sleep on their own. This is the most crucial element and from it stems all good practice. You should be able to leave your child in her cot or bed awake and let her go to sleep. Children will naturally wake during the night but they should be able to resettle themselves without having to wake you up for comfort, cuddles or company until they go back to sleep.[1]

If your child has problems either going to sleep in the first place or waking in the night, you should consider whether or not she is actually able to go to sleep on her own. Look at her sleep routine and see if she has formed a habit of only falling asleep in certain circumstances e.g. when you are present, if she has a bottle, if she is in your bed or if watching TV. If this is the case, then when she is waking in the night she cannot get back to sleep because she has not got her particular prop. You will have to tackle the 'going to sleep' routine as well as waking in the night.

The practice of sleep training
Bed-time routine

Establish a good routine before bed, for example a bath, a book and then bed. Don't make it overlong and don't play rough and tumble games which will excite and stimulate her. Make it soothing, relaxing and comforting.

When it is time to leave her, say goodnight and leave in a confident way. Mean business.

Ensure that the problem is not a practical one. Check that she is not too hot or too cold (continental-style sleeping-bag pyjamas or an extra layer of fleecy all-in-ones are good ways of keeping warm a child who always kicks off her blankets). Make sure she is not hungry at night by offering extra milk or something filling like a fromage frais at tea time. Some children with sensory integration disorder are very aware of how their bedclothes feel – the texture and the weight – so some might like to feel very

---

1   Polke, L. and Thompson, M. (eds) (1994) *Sleep and Settling Problems in Young Children.* Southampton Community NHS Trust, Child and Family Guidance Service for the Under Fives.

weighed down with heavy blankets and others might feel the opposite.

Settling down

If your child will not settle on her own, there are two main strategies. Choose the one which best suits your situation and temperament.

1. Once you have settled your child leave her. If she gets up just keep taking her back to bed saying 'time for bed'. You will have to carry on doing this for as long as it takes. The first night it may be twenty times but the next night it may be only a few because once she has learned that she is not going to gain anything she will give up and go to sleep.

    If your child is in a cot still and stands up and wails on being left, check and resettle her every five minutes or so (extending the time to ten and fifteen minutes) until she goes to sleep.

2. Alternatively, you can sit with your child until she falls asleep but each night position yourself further away from her. To begin with sit on the bed, then the next day on the floor by the bed, then further away until you are in the doorway, then on the landing, then just upstairs or nearby until she falls asleep on her own.

    > Jessica had been brilliant at sleeping in her cot but when she transferred to a bed, we had got into the habit of sitting with her until she fell asleep. It was fine until Steve started falling asleep with her only to wake an hour later feeling dreadful. The first night Steve sat on the floor, Jessica was hysterical and it turned out that that was the crucial change. We weathered that and then after three days of sitting further away Steve left her on her own and she has been fine ever since.

To make things easier, you could also try settling your child late, when she is really tired and then gradually bring her bedtime forwards by fifteen minutes each day until it reaches an acceptable time.

The crucial point is that you must not give in to your child. If you let your child cry for an hour and then give in to her, you will have taught her that if she cries enough she will get what she wants. So then the next night she will cry for an hour confident

that if she goes on long enough you will give in. You want to teach her the opposite – that you are resolute and she will do better to co-operate.

If your child is crying and you find it disturbing, go and find something to do which will distract you, even if it is just the washing up with the radio on.

Waking in the night

Usually children who wake in the night and need to be resettled are those who are unable to fall asleep on their own in their own bed. If you have successfully solved the problem of settling, you will probably also solve the problem of waking in the night. All children, however, may be disturbed by nightmares, coughs, itchiness or other illnesses from time to time but you should be able to go to their room, reassure them and leave promptly.

If your child continues to wake in the night, you should think about the rewards you may be giving her intentionally or unintentionally. It might be a kiss and a stroke, a drink, a cuddle, a visit to your bed or even games. You must stop those rewards. Once your child realizes that she is not going to gain anything by waking up in the night she will stop. There are two approaches to stopping rewards:

1. Stop all rewards immediately. If she wakes, put her to bed, tell her to 'go to sleep', give no eye contact and just check every five minutes that all is okay.

2. Alternatively, gradually reduce the rewards until she is going back to sleep on her own. For instance, if she is used to a cuddle you could give a very quick cuddle and then put her down, gradually reducing the cuddling over time until it is just a kiss or a pat and then nothing. If she is used to a drink of milk, give water instead and then nothing.

We tried the gradual approach with Nicholas, who at eight months had got so used to having a nice breastfeed and cuddle in the night that he continued to wake up even though he was not really hungry. One night we offered him a drink of water instead but he was not interested at all so then we just left him to cry and checked on him occasionally. Within a few days he was sleeping through the night.

Getting into parents' bed

Children love getting into their parents' bed for a cuddle and play before they get up in the morning. If you are happy for your children to do that then all is fine. However, it is better, if you want to establish a good sleep routine, not to have them sleeping in your bed, even for a short time.

If your child gets into bed with you in the middle of the night then you should take her straight back to her own bed with the minimum of fuss and eye contact and keep repeating this for as long as it takes for her to give up and go to sleep.

Some children can be extraordinarily quiet and can get into your bed in the middle of the night without your even realizing it. If your child does this often you can devise something to alert you, a bell on a closed door, for example, and then take her straight back to bed.

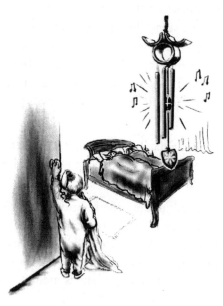

Devise something to alert you

Children who wake too early

If your child wakes too early you should try to ignore her, perhaps leaving her until a little bit later each day until you reach a time that is acceptable to you. You can put some interesting and special toys in her room and place a stair-gate across the entrance so that she cannot get out. Additionally, if your child has the understanding, have a radio, alarm or light which, when it comes on, is the signal that it is okay to get up. In the summer when it is light very early, children can be woken by the light and think it is time to get up. You can try blacking out the window with extra sheeting or curtain lining.

Daytime naps

Some children, like adults, find that a daytime sleep gives them enough of an energy boost so that they do not go to sleep at bed-time. Others are the opposite and find it difficult to sleep if they are too tired. Observe your child's patterns and see whether she sleeps better with or without a daytime nap. If she sleeps better with a nap, plan one into your daily routine. If on the other hand a nap keeps her up late, try to avoid giving her opportunities to fall asleep such as watching television or taking long drives in the late afternoon.

Good beginnings

If you have a very young baby who still needs to feed in the night, you can still start establishing good practice by making sure that at least sometimes she is put in her cot awake and left to fall asleep on her own and that you go to her at night rather than bring her into your bed.

Other points

- If your child is ill, forget about good sleep practice and just wait till she is fully recovered before starting again.

- If you are following the above approach without success, it may be because you are not identifying your child's reward for waking up. Think very carefully about what your child is getting out of waking up.

- Some families find themselves gradually developing extraordinary routines in order to get their children to sleep. If you find yourself in this situation, you will probably need to talk to an outsider to help you change your approach.

- If you have fears and anxieties about your child, they are much more likely to surface at night time and they may stop you from feeling able to leave your child at night. You may need help to address those issues before you can deal with sleep problems.

TOILET TRAINING

When your child is showing some awareness that she is weeing or pooing in her nappy, is doing proper wees rather than continual dribbles and perhaps showing some interest in using the potty or toilet, start to think about toilet training

Toilet training is one of the most emotive areas of child development. Do not get upset about it. There is a huge variation in the ages when ordinary children are ready for potty training, let alone children with special needs. Other parents will talk about their own child's successes and you may feel pressure to start toilet training, particularly from people of the older generation who tried to potty train earlier. Ignore them and think only of your child, her needs and development stage.

As well as your child being ready you must think of your own needs:

- Think about what toilet training will mean for you. Changing nappies is one thing but clearing up soiled pants and mopping up puddles can really get you down. You must not show any annoyance with your child and it can be quite difficult. Make sure you are in a mood to handle it.

- Try it at a settled time when there are no major emotional disruptions such as a new baby or a trip away. It will be easier for you and your child.

- It is much easier to potty train in your own home, when you are not out and about too much and haven't got to worry about other people's expensive carpets.

Preparations and practical arrangements

Make life as easy as possible for everyone:

- There will be a lot of washing and a lot of clearing up. Summer is therefore easier because washing dries quicker, children wear less and you can do a lot of potty training outside.

- Make sure your child is wearing clothes which are easy to remove, like pull-on trousers rather than dungarees.

- Buy lots of pairs of pants as you will get through masses each day to begin with.

- A period when your child is on holiday from playgroup is often a good time to start as you can stay at home more easily and get people to come to you. If your child goes to a playgroup, school or childminder, keep them informed and get them to use the same method.

- Use either a potty or training seat, whatever suits your child. To begin with take it everywhere with you as your child will probably not be able to give you much warning. For example, have a potty downstairs, upstairs and in the car or pushchair when you go out. Specialist equipment is available from occupational therapists if you need it.

The theory

Once you start you should not stop but persist, however long it takes. However, if you find you have misjudged the timing and your child is clearly not ready, stop, go back to nappies and try again in three to six months' time.

You must praise successes to the skies and ignore failures

Be as relaxed as possible. It is important not to get cross or to show any kind of annoyance or frustration at having to clear up mess because it can be counter-productive, making your child upset and unco-operative.

You need a word, sign or symbol to indicate 'toilet'. It might be the word toilet or wee, or you could use the Makaton sign or your own personal sign or word. Eventually you will want it to be generally understood. If your child does not yet understand a sign or word you will need to give her one. Every time she goes on the potty or toilet make the sign or say the word and keep reinforcing it. Tell other people who care for her what her sign or word for toilet is.

> My son used the sign for horse because we live in the New Forest and there is a lot of horse dung around so he made an association between horse and poo! After a few months he picked up the proper sign for toilet.

Be patient

It may take days, weeks or months. However long it takes there may be lapses for a long time afterwards. Changes of routine, too much excitement, illness, different drinks and different environments can make toilet training go to pot (if you will excuse the pun) for a few hours or days.

The practice

Show your child what to do. Take her to the toilet with you and show her your wee and poo. You can even use the potty yourself for a bit.

Put your child on the potty when you think you might have some success. For instance, if you know she always does a poo after lunch, take her nappy off and put her on the potty then. See what success you have.

At some point, however, you will have to take the plunge, stop using nappies altogether and put your child on the potty, either when you think you might have some success or very frequently (maybe every half an hour to begin with).

Ignore accidents totally and don't get upset if she doesn't do anything on the potty. When your child does do something in the potty praise her excessively, if possible get the whole family to admire her achievements. Really overdo the praise with smiles, clapping, shouting etc.

As a parent you may be able to recognize that your child wants to go the loo by her body language such as scratching the groin or manic behaviour. Use those clues.

That's all there is to it. You just want to catch some poo or wee, praise her and the praise will encourage your child to repeat her achievement when she is placed on the potty.

Initially, you will control when your child goes on the potty. It is a nuisance for you to be forever remembering to put her on the potty but it is also a pain for your child so she will learn to say 'no' when you suggest it and she is not interested.

> My son used to pull his trousers straight back up again and then learnt vehement head shaking as a response to 'Do you want the potty?'

Eventually, your child will be able to tell you that she wants to use the toilet but initially she will only be able to give you short notice. Even if it's too late, never mind, just praise her for telling you. Gradually she will recognize her needs more easily and give you more notice. Carry a potty with you everywhere and don't be embarrassed about getting it out and using it in public. It is a lot easier than dealing with a child who has wet or soiled pants.

Points to remember

Sometimes it can be very difficult to get a child to sit on the potty at all. Try entertaining her with something she loves – reading books, singing games or blowing bubbles – to get her on the potty and to keep her there for a few minutes.

When you start potty training it is tempting to put nappies back on when you go out, but ultimately you have to make the commitment to toilet training and remove them totally. It is too confusing for a child to work out that when she has nappies on she can wee in her nappy but when she hasn't she must wee in the potty.

If your child soils her pants make sure you clean the poo into the potty to reinforce that the 'poo goes in the potty not your pants'.

Watch out that you don't make a reward out of failure. Some children love seeing all the fuss involved with clearing up the mess. If that is the case, exclude your child from the scene as quickly as you can without upsetting her and then clean up.

Some children learn to wee in the potty first, some to poo first and some to do both simultaneously. There is no right or wrong order. There is nothing you can do but be patient.

If your child's toilet training seems to be going backwards increase the level of praise again to regain momentum. It could be that you have got out of the habit of praising success.

Dry at night

There is not much you can do to make your child dry at night except wait for her to do it by herself. If you notice her nappy is dry consistently in the mornings remove nappies at night and see what happens. Try the following ideas to establish a good routine or if things start going wrong:

- Put your child on the potty last thing at night and first thing in the morning.
- If she wets her bed at around waking-up time, set your alarm for thirty minutes earlier than normal and get her up to wee in the potty to re-establish the routine. Once dry again gradually move the alarm setting back.

- Leave a potty in her bedroom so she can easily get up to use it.

- In the winter when it is very dark your child may not want to get up to use the toilet. Leave a low-wattage light on somewhere useful so that she can see her way to the toilet confidently.

- Use mattress liners and half sheets to ease changing wet sheets in the middle of the night.

- Use star charts and other rewards if your child has the necessary level of understanding.

CHAPTER 10

The Support Your Child Should Expect

SUPPORT FROM HEALTH, EDUCATION AND SOCIAL SERVICES

This section lists the different health and education professionals with whom you may have contact. Provision varies enormously according to where you live and you may well have to push to get the level of provision that you think your child needs. It is also often difficult for parents to find out what support is available so again parents have to ask and probe to get the necessary information. The statutory assessment process is covered below, see pages 220–222.

I have described the different professionals, what they do, the manner in which they work and how to get a referral, but again their roles and organization do vary.

When dealing with professionals

Always remember that you as a parent know your child far better than anyone else. You must have the confidence and courage to make demands and decisions about your child. You know far better than any professional what your child's abilities are, where he has problems, where he needs help and when things are not working. The professionals are there to support and help you and your child but they are not the experts on him. Have confidence in your views and tell the professionals what you think because they want to know this. A true partnership between parent and professional will generate the best provision.

Try to create good relationships with professionals. Inevitably you will get more help, advice and support and it will come much easier if you communicate well. Resources in most areas are constrained and therefore you often have to push, nag and fight for services but you can do this while maintaining friendly relations.

If you are going to an important consultation with a professional, write down any questions you have before you go, because you may find you forget everything when you are on the spot. Also take someone along with you to help look after your child during the meeting. This will allow you to concentrate on talking to the professional and you can get the other person to help you remember what was said afterwards.

Professionals
General practitioner (GP)

GPs are often the first point of contact for parents with concerns about their child's health and development. GPs are then able to refer children on to more specialist services if they think it necessary. They provide on-going support and advice to you and your child and should be an advocate for your child, ensuring he gets the services he needs.

Health visitor

All children have a health visitor through their GP surgery. Health visitors have a special role in following the development of children usually from about ten days old. The health visitor, together with the GP, carries out developmental checks at about 6 weeks, 8 months, 18 months–2 years and 3–3½ years and is always available for parents if they have concerns about health or child-care issues like feeding, behaviour, toileting, sleep etc.

Health visitors can make referrals for parents to GPs, speech and language therapists, dieticians, audiologists etc.

Paediatrician

The paediatrician is a doctor who specializes in children's health. He or she has an overall responsibility for your child's development and should ensure that he gets the support and services he needs.

Children can be referred by their GP.

Occupational therapist (OT)

OTs who work with young children are concerned with the following areas: fine motor and gross motor skills, seating and positioning, toileting, feeding, dressing, general play and perceptual skills.

They work with parents to establish a programme of activities which parents can work on and they provide equipment for feeding or seating to aid the child's development.

The frequency with which an OT will see your child is dependent on his needs. It may be a weekly or fortnightly visit or it may be an occasional visit to address a specific problem.

OTs work with pre-school children at home, opportunity groups, nurseries and child development centres. They may give school-age children a programme of activities to do at school but there should still be liaison with parents.

Children can be referred by their GP or paediatrician.

Physiotherapist

Physiotherapists are concerned with the physical development of people. They are always concerned with gross motor movements and in some health authorities cover fine motor skills as well (in others these are handled by the occupational therapist).

They usually work with parents to assess a child's physical needs and draw up long-term and short-term goals. They work on physical activities with the child and give parents a programme of activities for them to work on.

The provision varies according to the child. Some may need regular physiotherapy for many years while others may need an intensive period only or to be seen only occasionally.

Pre-school children can seen at home, at nursery or at a child development centre. Once a child starts school his programme may be incorporated into his school activities but parents should be involved.

Children can be referred by their GP or paediatrician.

Speech and language therapist

Speech and language therapists work with children on helping communication skills. In some health authorities they also work on eating skills. They assess a child and then draw up a programme of activities for parents, schools or other staff to work on with the child on a regular basis. They review a child's progress according to need.

Children can be referred by their paediatrician, GP or health visitor etc.

Educational psychologist (EdPsych or EP)

Educational psychologists assess children with special needs by looking at their play skills and communication skills and discussing these with their parents. They may then make recommendations of the type of provision children need, for example, portage or a nursery placement and can suggest targets and strategies appropriate for individual children. Educational psychologists play a crucial role in the statutory assessment of a child and can initiate one if necessary.

Children can be referred by their paediatrician, health visitor, speech and language therapist or parents directly.

Portage home visitor

Portage is a home-based scheme for pre-school children which is based on a partnership with parents. A portage home visitor visits your home on a weekly or fortnightly basis for about an hour to play with your child. Every six months, the parents and home visitor decide on a list of goals for your child and will then work towards achieving them. Each week the home visitor draws up an activity chart for parents and the parents carry out a specified activity each day and record the child's response. Progress is very carefully monitored. To be eligible a child usually has to have problems in more than one area of development.

Parents can be referred by their GP, health visitor or paediatrician.

Sight and hearing advisers

They provide support, help, advice and ideas for parents of children who are visually or hearing impaired on games, activities and practical issues. They visit homes and schools.

Social worker

Social workers can provide support for parents of children with special needs, for instance respite care (see below p.226), summer holiday play schemes, help in the home and equipment for the house if you have a child who is always trying to escape.

If a family uses any of the services they may have a full assessment of their needs made but often this is not deemed necessary.

If parents want to use any of the services offered they should contact their local social services department within their local authority (see your local phone book for a telephone number and address).

Services

Opportunity group

These are playgroups for children with special needs, sometimes their siblings and other children. They vary enormously in the way they are run. Some have no staff but provide an opportunity for parents to bring their children together to play. Others have paid or voluntary staff who provide one-on-one support for the children and will work on programmes such as portage, OT and physio and give parents respite. Some have input directly from professionals.

They are usually run by a voluntary committee of parents, are registered by social services and are members of the Pre-school Learning Alliance.

Children can be referred by their GP, health visitor or paediatrician.

Child development centre

Some health authorities run child development centres which children with special needs attend at least once a week. All the therapists and the paediatrician attend regularly. It has the advantage that assessments and therapy happen in one place instead of different locations. Because different services attend together they are able to communicate more effectively with each other. It is also an opportunity for parents to meet others in a similar position. Because it is a familiar environment, children are able to feel confident and comfortable when they are being assessed. Children may attend just for a short assessment period or for a longer duration.

Children can be referred by their paediatrician or therapists.

STATUTORY ASSESSMENT OR THE STATEMENTING PROCESS

If your child has special needs which are identified pre-school, he may need to be assessed to ensure that when he starts school at four or five his special needs are properly identified and addressed by the teachers, school and local education authority (LEA). This process is called the statutory assessment of special educational needs (SEN) and may result in a statement of special educational needs so it is often called 'statementing'.

If your child is already at school, he would normally go through a number of stages of assessment (1–3) aimed at addressing his needs within the school before a statutory assessment (stage 4) can be requested.

Statementing is a very complex, detailed and lengthy process which is carried out by your local education authority, but the aim is to identify your child's particular needs for education – for example, speech therapy or physiotherapy – and the best school for him. Only a small proportion of children will have needs that require a statement. The majority of children with special educational needs will be supported through stages 1–3 in a mainstream school.

You have two main responsibilities:

1. To give as much detailed information about your child as you can, so that the LEA can make an informed judgement.

2. To consider all schools which might be appropriate, and decide which you think would be best for your child.

The procedure

You can apply for a statutory assessment at any time as long as no assessment has been undertaken in the previous six months. A statutory assessment is unusual for a child under two but if requested the LEA must undertake such an assessment. LEA and health authorities should liaise to identify pre-school children who may require an assessment prior to school entry and therefore an assessment would usually be made as a child is approaching school age.

There is an initial form to complete in which you should give a brief description of your child, his educational progress and the professionals involved. From this and other information and

evidence the LEA will decide if there are sufficient grounds to proceed with a statutory assessment.

If the LEA decide to proceed they gather reports from all professionals involved with your child (for example teachers, educational psychologists, paediatricians, social services, physiotherapists, occupational therapists, speech therapists, opportunity group and portage, etc). You are requested to provide an assessment of your child's development and give your views on his educational needs.

The LEA will then consider the reports it receives and may draw up a draft statement. This will give details of your child's special educational needs, the provision required to meet them, the long-term educational objectives and the non-educational needs and provision that he requires.

You should consider the content of the draft statement and request a meeting with the LEA within two weeks if you are seeking clarification, changes, amendments or additions to the draft statement. In addition, at this stage you can make representations and/or express preferences for the school which you want your child to attend.

Once agreed the LEA will then issue the final statement which will state the school your child will attend. The LEA then have a statutory obligation to fulfil the requirements of the statement. If your child moves, the statement will go with him and the new LEA will inherit the statutory obligations but have the opportunity to request a revision.

A statement is reviewed at least annually involving parents and appropriate professional staff.

Time-scale

The time-limit for undertaking a statutory assessment is 26 weeks but it may take a shorter or longer period depending on circumstances.

Appeal

There are rights of appeal for parents against decisions made by the LEA. See *The Code of Practice on the Identification and Assessment of Special Educational Needs,* available from the Department for Education and Employment.

Selecting a school

As soon as you embark on the statutory assessment you should start looking at possible schools. Try to approach schools with an open mind, think what would suit your child at that particular time and try not to be too prejudiced for or against one particular form of education. There are three main types of school: mainstream, special and independent. You need to work out in which environment your child would thrive by considering the issues below:

- local vs. non-local (part of the local community, distance to travel);
- integration vs. segregation (learning alongside 'normal' children, role models, teasing);
- experienced staff vs. general classroom teachers (specialist experience, training in special needs, access to therapists);
- facilities (access to riding, hydrotherapy, sensory rooms).

The above is a very brief resumé of statementing. For more detailed information request a free copy of *Special Educational Needs: A Guide for Parents* and *The Code of Practice on the Identification and Assessment of Special Educational Needs* issued by the Department for Education and Employment. Contact tel: 0845 602 2260 or fax: 0845 603 3360.

It is possible that your LEA has a parent partnership service which can assist parents with the statementing process and also provide parents with advice, guidance and information. Contact your LEA to find the number. Many voluntary organizations also produce useful guides to the statementing process. Contact such organizations as Mencap, ACE and Network 81 or the voluntary organization specific to your own child's special needs listed in Chapter 11, pages 233–254.

SOURCES OF SUPPORT – FINANCE, EQUIPMENT AND RESPITE

Having a child with special needs can lead to considerable extra costs, so listed below are some of the sources of support available.

Social security benefits

There are various social security benefits you can claim for your child and for the main carer. These are in addition to child benefit which, as with all children, you are entitled to for each of your children.

Your local Citizens Advice Bureau can always advise people on their rights. Look in your telephone directory for their address and phone number.

Disability Living Allowance (DLA)

This is an allowance for people or children who need help with personal care, with getting around, or both. There are two components:

1. Care (for extra and additional care) available from birth paid at three rates:

   - High – for people/children who need help both day and night;
   - Middle – for people/children who need help during the day or night;
   - Low – for people/children who need some help during the day.

2. Mobility (for help getting around) only available from five years old, paid at two rates:

   - Higher – for people/children unable or virtually unable to walk;
   - Lower – for people/children who need someone to provide them with guidance and supervision for most of the time they are outdoors in unfamiliar surroundings.

The DLA forms have recently been improved so that they are relevant to young children, but the information emphasizes how your child must require much more care than an ordinary child. For some parents who are just learning to cope with their child's needs it may be very disturbing to have to stress their child's difficulties all the time.

Nevertheless, fill in the forms with as much information as you can. If you feel that the questions are not very helpful add a statement of your own describing your child's needs at home and describing all the extra things you have to do – medical care, extra care for feeding and bathing, travelling time to appointments and playgroups, extra washing, additional play, physio, OT, speech, portage programmes etc.

An adjudication officer at the Department of Social Security will decide on whether you qualify and for which category – Low, Middle or High. You can ask for a review if you are not happy with the decision. You must write and request it within three months and enclose any additional information. If you are still not happy with the decision you can go to appeal.

The criteria by which they judge cases can seem a bit odd so it is well worth giving as much information as possible to sell your case and help them make their decision. It is also worth asking for a revision if you feel the decision has been unfair.

Contact the Benefit Enquiry Line on 0800 882200 for an application form. Your local Citizens Advice Bureau will give you advice on completing the forms and on any appeals. Your social worker should be able to help and many voluntary organizations like the RNIB and the National Deaf Children's Society give good advice and information.

Invalid Care Allowance (ICA)

This allowance is for those who are of working age and care for a child who gets Disability Living Allowance care component at the higher or middle rate. You must be caring for the child for at least 35 hours a week and earning not more than £50 per week after deduction of taxable allowances. The Allowance is taxable. The application form is very straightforward.

To obtain a form contact the Benefit Enquiry Line on 0800 882200.

If you have other people to support, such as children or a partner, you may be able to get more than the basic rate but it depends on other earnings and benefits you may be getting.

If you receive income support you can claim ICA with an extra carer's premium but your income support will be reduced by the basic amount of the ICA.

If you receive ICA you automatically get credited with national insurance contributions so that your pension is protected.

Additional financial support

The following organizations provide extra financial support in more specific cases.

Family Fund Trust
PO Box 50
York YO1 9ZX
Tel: 01904 621115

Aims to ease the stress on families who care for a very severely disabled child under 16 by providing grants and information. Gives financial grants which relate directly to the child's needs, e.g. for help with play equipment, extra laundry, getting around, holidays or outings etc. Assistance can only be given to those families whose gross income is less than £18,800 (1998 figures) and have no more than £8000 in savings. For more information and an application form contact the above address. Also produces a range of publications on such issues as 'Adaptations to Housing', 'Bedding and Clothing', 'Hearing Impairment' and 'Holidays'.

Family Welfare Association
501–505 Kingsland Road
Dalston
London E8 4AU
Tel: 0171 254 6251
Fax: 0171 249 5443

Can provide one-off grants to anyone living in the UK who is in need of financial assistance at a time of crisis in their lives. Money can be given for a range of needs such as clothing, fuel bills and household items. It can also help with more unusual items such as electronic communication aids. Council tax, rent arrears, fines etc. cannot be covered. Grants are usually between £100 and £200. Applications are made through a health visitor, social worker or Citizens Advice Bureau.

Other support
Orange badge scheme

You can apply for an orange badge to allow you to park in disabled parking spaces or on yellow lines if you are out with a disabled person. Your child must be over two years old. Contact your local social services.

Free nappies

If your child is still in nappies at three years old you can apply for free nappies from your local health authority. Contact your health visitor.

Pushchairs

You may be able to have the loan of a single or double pushchair if your child still needs one when he is two years and six months. Contact your health visitor, GP or occupational therapist.

Respite care

Social services have a variety of schemes to give parents of children with special needs some respite care. You may need some time without your child so that, for example, you can have a break, go to appointments, shop or spend some time with your other children or your partner.

Respite care is offered under a number of schemes and seems to be organized flexibly to fit with parents' needs – a day per week or month, overnight stays, weekend breaks, extra help in school holidays. Respite carers have all been checked by social services and will provide a family environment for your child. Social services will often provide necessary equipment for the carer. You usually have to take your child to the carer. Some social services departments make a charge.

Contact your local social services to find out about schemes known as Family Link Schemes, Family Help Schemes or Family Support Services.

SNAPS – Special Needs Annual Play Schemes

Many social services departments and voluntary organizations, notably MENCAP and the National Childrens Home, run play schemes for children with special needs during the summer holidays. These provide both enjoyable and educational experiences for children and respite for parents. Contact social services or enquire locally to find out what is available in your area.

Alterations to houses

Remember that local authorities have powers to make grants for alterations to houses to adapt them for disabled people and children over five. The rules are complex so contact your local authority for details.

Cars and wheelchairs

Motability, which is a non-profit making organization, runs a scheme to enable those in receipt of the higher rate Mobility Component of Disability Living Allowance to lease or buy a car. They operate schemes which help those who need to pay for adaptations to cars including the Government's grant scheme (Mobility Equipment Fund). To qualify for the higher rate Mobility Component of DLA a child must be over five years old (see above), so bear it in mind for the future.

Motability also operate a hire purchase scheme for wheelchairs. Contact:

Motability
Goodman House
Station Approach
Harlow
Essex CM20 2ET
Tel: 01279 635999.

CHAPTER 11

Resources

BIBLIOGRAPHY

Attention Deficit Disorder (ADD)

Flick, G.L. (1998) *ADD/ADHD Behavior Change Resource Kit: Ready to Use Strategies and Activities for Helping Children with ADD.* New York: Center for Applied Research in Education.

Jones, C.B. (1991) *Sourcebook for Children with ADD.* San Antonio, Texas: Communication Skill Builders.

Autism

Alvin, J. and Warwick, A. (1994) *Music Therapy for the Autistic Child.* Oxford: Oxford University Press.

Amenta, C.A. (1992) *Russell is Extra Special: A Book about Autism for Children.* New York: Magination Press.

Attwood, T. (1993) *Why Does Chris Do That?* London: National Autistic Society.

Baron-Cohen, S. and Bolton, P. (1993) *Autism: The Facts.* Oxford: Oxford University Press.

Powers, M.D. (1989) *Children with Autism: A Parents' Guide.* Rockville, MD: Woodbine House.

Schopler, E. (ed) (1995) *Parent Survival Manual: A Guide To Crisis Resolution in Autism and Related Development Disorders.* New York: Plenum Press.

Wing, L. (1989) *The Autistic Spectrum: A Guide for Parents and Professionals.* London: Constable and Co. Ltd.

Behaviour management

Phelan, T.W. (1995) *1–2–3 Magic: Effective Discipline for Children 2–12.* Glen Ellyn, ILL: Child Management Inc.

Cerebral palsy

Boos, M.L., Duffy, L., Pearson, D.T., Walter, R.S. and Whinston, J.L. (1995) *Cerebral Palsy: A Complete Guide for Caregiving.* Johns Hopkins University Press.

Cogher, L., Savage, E. and Smith, M.F. (eds) (1992) *Cerebral Palsy – The Child and Young Person.* London: Chapman & Hall.

Finnie, N.R. (1997) *Handling the Young Child with Cerebral Palsy at Home.* Oxford: Butterworth Heinemann.

Geralis, E. (ed) (1991) *Children With Cerebral Palsy: A Parent's Guide.* Rockville, MD: Woodbine House.

Griffiths, M. and Clegg, M. (1988) *Cerebral Palsy – Problems and Practice.* London: Souvenir Press.

Miller, F. and Bachrach, S.J. (1995) *Cerebral Palsy – A Complete Guide to Caregiving.* Baltimore: Johns Hopkins University Press.

Stranton, M. (1992) *Cerebral Palsy: A Practical Handbook for Families and Carers.* London: Vermilion.

Child development

Bruce, T. (1996) *Helping Young Children to Play.* London: Hodder & Stoughton.

Lansdown, R. and Walker, M. (1991) *Your Child's Development from Birth to Adolescence.* Frances Lincoln Ltd.

Leach, P. (1974) *Babyhood.* London: Penguin.

Lee, C. (1990) *Growth and Development of Children.* Harlow: Longman.

Minnett, P. (1985) *Child Care and Development.* London: John Murrray.

Natanson, J. (1997) *Learning through Play.* London: Ward Lock.

Sheridan, M.D. (1993) *From Birth to Five Years, Children's Developmental Progress.* London: Routledge.

Down's Syndrome

Buckley, S., Emslie, M. and Haslegrave, G. (1993) *The Development of Language and Reading Skills in Children with Down's Syndrome.* Portsmouth: University of Portsmouth.

Cairo, S. (1985) *Our Brother has Down's Syndrome.* Toronto: Annic Press.

Cicchetti, D. and Beeghly, M. (1990) *Children with Down's Syndrome: A Developmental Perspective.* Cambridge: Cambridge University Press.

Cunningham, C. (1990) *Down's Syndrome: An Introduction for Parents.* London: Souvenir Press.

Hanson, M.J. (1995) *Teaching the Infant with Down's Syndrome: Manual of Ideas.* Delray Beach, FL: Winslow Press.

Kumin, L. (1994) *Communication Skills in Children with Down's Syndrome.* Rockville, MD: Woodbine House.

Mepsted, J. (1996) *Developing the Child with Down's Syndrome.* Plymouth: Northcote House.

Pueschel, S.M. (1990) *A Parent's Guide to Down's Syndrome.* Baltimore, MD: Paul Brookes Publishing Co.

Stray-Gunderson, K. (1995) *Babies with Down's Syndrome: A New Parents' Guide.* Rockville, MD: Woodbine House.

Thompson, M. (1992) *My Brother Matthew.* Rockville, MD: Woodbine House.

Dyspraxia

Barrett, J., Daines, B. and Ripley, K. (1997) *Dyspraxia and Motor Planning: A Guide for Parents and Teachers.* London: David Fulton.

Cocks, N. (1996) *Watch Me I Can Do It: Helping Children Overcome Clumsy and Unco-ordinated Motor Skills.* London: Simon & Schuster (originally known as *Skipping Not Tripping*).

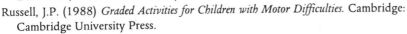

Penso, D. (1992) *Perceptuo-Motor Difficulties: Theories and Strategies to Help Children, Adolescents and Adults.* Cheltenham: Stanley Thorne.

Portwood, M. (1996) *Developmental Dyspraxia.* Durham County Council (available from Educational Psychology Service, Greencroft, Neville's Cross, Durham DH1 4UH, tel: 0191-384 0707).

Russell, J.P. (1988) *Graded Activities for Children with Motor Difficulties.* Cambridge: Cambridge University Press.

Epilepsy

Reisner, H. (1988) *Children with Epilepsy: A Parents Guide.* Rockville, MD: Woodbine House.

Hearing impaired

Courtman, D.M. (1979) *Your Deaf Child's Speech and Language.* London: Bodley Head.

Gregory, S. (1995) *Deaf Children and their Families.* Cambridge: Cambridge University Press.

Fletcher, L. (1987) *Language for Ben.* London: Souvenir Press.

Lindquist, I. (1977) *Therapy through Play.* London: Arlington Books.

Lynas, W. (1990) *A Current Review of Approaches to Communication in the Education of Deaf Children.* Ewing Foundation (available from The Ewing Foundation, c/o Centre for Audiology, Education of the Deaf and Speech Pathology, University of Manchester, Oxford Road, Manchester M13 9PL).

McCracken, W. and Sutherland, H. (1991) *Deafability not Disability: Guide for Parents of Hearing Impaired Children.* Clevedon: Multilingual Matters.

Nolan, M. and Tucker, I. (1988) *The Hearing Impaired Child and Family.* London: Souvenir Press.

Smith, C. (1992) *Signs Make Sense.* London: Souvenir Press.

Play ideas

Britton, L. (1992) *Montessori Play and Learn: A Parent's Guide to Purposeful Play from 2–6.* London: Vermilion.

Denziloe, J. (1994) *Fun and Games: Practical Leisure Ideas for People with Profound Disabilities.* Oxford: Butterworth Heinemann.

Einon, D. (1985) *Creative Play.* London: Penguin.

Gee, R. and Meredith, S. (1993) *Entertaining and Educating your Preschool Child.* London: Usborne.

Hong, C.S., Gabriel, H. and St John, C. (1996) *Sensory Motor Activities for Early Development.* Bicester, Oxon: Winslow Press.

Hornsby, B. (1989) *Before Alpha Learning Games for the Under 5s.* London: Souvenir Press.

Jeffree, D. and McConkey, R. (1976) *Let Me Speak.* London: Souvenir Press.

Jeffree, D., McConkey, R. and Hewson, S. (1994) *Let Me Play.* London: Souvenir Press.

Jeffree, D., McConkey, R. and Hewson, S. (1977) *Teaching the Handicapped Child.* London: Souvenir Press.

Jeffree, D. and McConkey, R. (1981) *Let's Make Toys.* London: Souvenir Press.

Johansson, I. (1994) *Language Development in Children with Special Needs – Performative Communication.* London: Jessica Kingsley Publishers.

Lear, R. (1996) *Play Helps*. Oxford: Butterworth Heinemann.

Lear, R. (1998) *Look at It This Way: Toys and Activities for Children with a Visual Impairment*. London: Heinemann.

Lynch, C. and Cooper, J. (1991) *Early Communication Skills*. Bicester, Oxon: Winslow Press.

Matteson, E. (1989) *Play with a Purpose for the Under Sevens*. London: Penguin.

Nash-Wortham, M. and Hunt, J. (1994) *Take Time: Movement Exercises for Parents, Teachers and Therapists of Children with Difficulties in Speaking, Reading, Writing and Spelling*. Stourbridge: Robinswood Press.

National Association of Toy and Leisure Libraries (1989) *Talk to Me*. London: NATLL.

National Association of Toy and Leisure Libraries (1990) *Switch to Play*. London: NATLL.

Rice, M. (1993) *Child's Play*. London: Kingfisher Books.

Riddick, B. (1982) *Toys and Play for the Handicapped*. London: Croom Helm.

Schwartz, S. (1988) *The New Language of Toys: Teaching Communication Skills to Children with Special Needs*. Rockville, MD: Woodbine House.

Shaw, C. (1993) *Talking and Your Child*. London: Hodder & Stoughton.

Streeter, E. (1993) *Making Music with the Young Child with Special Needs*. London: Jessica Kingsley Publishers.

Winders, P.C. (1997) *Gross Motor Skills in Children with Down Syndrome*. Rockville, MD: Woodbine House Inc.

Sensory integration disorder

Anderson, E. and Emmons, P. (1996) *Unlocking the Mysteries of Sensory Dysfunction*. Arlington: Future Horizons.

Kranowitz, C.S. (1998) *The Out of Sync Child: Recognizing and Coping with Sensory Integration Dysfunction*. New York: Skylight Press.

Trott, M.C. with Laurel, M.K. and Windeck, S.L. (1993) *Understanding Sensory Integration*. Tuscon: Therapy Skill Builders.

Sleep management

Durand, V.M. (1988) *Sleep Better! A Guide to Improving Sleep for Children with Special Needs*. Baltimore, MD: Paul H. Brookes.

Ferber, R. (1986) *Solve Your Child's Sleep Problems: A Practical and Comprehensive Guide for Parents*. London: Dorling Kindersley.

Special needs

Greenspan, S.I. and Wieder, S. with Simons, R. (1998) *The Child with Special Needs: Encouraging Intellectual and Emotional Growth*. Reading, MA: Merloyd Lawrence.

Hannaford, C. (1995) *Smart Moves: Why Learning Is Not All in Your Head*. Arlington: Great Ocean Publishers.

Kimpton, D. (1990) *A Special Child in the Family: Living with Your Sick or Disabled Child*. London: Sheldon Press.

Knight, A. (1996) *Caring for a Disabled Child*. London: Straightforward Publishing.

Serfontein, G. (1990) *Hidden Handicap: How to Help Children who Suffer from Dyslexia, Hyperactivity and Learning Difficulties*. London: Simon & Schuster.

Woolfson, R. (1991) *Children with Special Needs*. London: Faber & Faber Ltd.

Visually impaired

Sonksen, P. and Stiff, B. (1991) *Show Me What My Friends Can See: A Developmental Guide for Babies with Severely Impaired Sight and Their Professional Advisers.* London: Institute of Child Health.

RNIB/MENCAP (1995) *Play it My Way: Learning Through Play with Your Visually Impaired Child.* London: RNIB and MENCAP (for addresses see below).

Books of nursery rhymes and songs

Brown, M. (ed) (1994) *Play Rhymes.* London: Picture Lions (HarperCollins).

Beck, I. and Williams, S. (1986) *Round and Round the Garden.* Oxford: Oxford University Press.

Beck, I. and Williams, S. (1988) *Ride a Cock Horse.* Oxford: Oxford University Press.

Nicholls, S. (1992) *Bobby Shaftoe Clap Your Hands.* London: A&C Black Ltd.

Opie, I. and P. (1955) *Oxford Nursery Rhyme Book.* Oxford: Oxford University Press.

VOLUNTARY ORGANIZATIONS OFFERING SUPPORT FOR PARENTS OF CHILDREN WITH SPECIAL NEEDS

Listed below are national organizations which provide support and information for parents of children with special needs who are of pre-school age or just starting school. Both mainstream and alternative organizations are listed. I have focused on the services provided which are relevant to the pre-school age group rather than trying to describe in full everything the organizations do. You can always contact the organizations to request full details of what they do.

There are also many excellent local organizations and help groups which it is not practical to list here.

Most organizations provide information to parents free of charge even if they are not members. However, since membership costs are usually fairly nominal, it is often well worth joining the organization relevant to your child. Many of the organizations have comprehensive mail-order book catalogues and so are a good source of relevant books.

If your child has a disability not included in the lists, consult *The CaF Directory of Specific Conditions and Rare Syndromes in Children with their Family Support Networks* (most public libraries have a copy) which lists many more organizations. Alternatively contact the following charities which may be able to put you in touch with a support group or other parents whose children have the same condition.

Contact a Family

170 Tottenham Court Road
London W1P 0HA
Tel: 0171 383 3555
Fax: 0171 383 0259
E-mail: info@cafamily.org.uk
Website: www.cafamily.org.uk

For families of children with any type of special need. Provides advice and information and has a network of local and national support groups. Provides a particularly valuable service of linking up parents of children with very rare diseases and conditions.

In Touch

10 Norman Road
Sale
Cheshire M33 3DF
Tel: 0161 905 2440
Fax: 0161 718 5787
E-mail: jworth@globalnet.co.uk

For professionals and parents of children with special needs, particularly those with rare disorders. Will link parents up to the appropriate support group or if one does not exist to other families on an individual basis. Can also refer families to sources of advice and information on aspects of caring for a child with special needs. Publishes a newsletter with information on new developments, groups, publications and conferences.

The Undiagnosed Children's Group

Brook Hall
Hall Road
Asheldham
Southminster
Essex CM0 7JF
Tel: 01621 773906

For children who have had an undiagnosed disability from birth or who develop one during childhood and their families. Provides information, counselling and support. Also welcomes any family which has been unable to find a support group to join.

National organizations

The organizations below are listed alphabetically.

Action for Sick Children

Argyle House
29–31 Euston Road
London NW1 2SD
Tel: 0171 833 2041
Fax: 0171 837 2110
E-mail: action_for_ sick_children_edu@msh.com

Aims to raise standards of health care for all children whether at home or in hospital. Provides support and advice for parents with sick children through a national network and produces publications on *When your Child is Sick, Coming into Hospital* and *Children and Pain.* Campaigns to enable parents to have a greater role in their children's hospital care.

Advisory Centre for Education

Unit 1B Aberdeen Studios
22–24 Highbury Grove
London N5 2DQ
Tel: 0171 354 8321 (Mon–Fri, 2–5pm)
Fax: 0171 354 9069

Believes that children benefit from greater openness and accountability in education. Therefore encourages parents to become actively involved in their child's education. Produces a range of publications on school and education including *Special Education Handbook: The Law on Children with Special Needs.*

AFASIC (Association for all Speech Impaired Children)

347 Central Markets
Smithfield
London EC1A 9NH
Tel: 0171 236 3632 (helpline)
Tel: 0171 236 6487 (admin)
Fax: 0171 236 8115
E-mail: info@afasic.org.uk
Website: www.afasic.org.uk

Aims to help children and young adults with speech and language impairments. Provides information and support, organizes seminars and conferences and runs activity weeks for children and young people. Also has local groups of parents. Has a publications and video list including *Speech and Language Explained* and *Help your Child to Talk.*

Association for Spina Bifida and Hydrocephalus

ASBAH House
42 Park Road
Peterborough PE1 2UQ
Tel: 01733 555988
Fax: 01733 555985
E-mail: postmaster@asbah.demon.co.uk
Website: www.asbah.demon.co.uk

For individuals with spina bifida and/or hydrocephalus and their families. Provides advice, advocacy, information and other services. Publishes a bi-monthly magazine plus pamphlets, notably an information pack for new parents which covers such issues as developing skills through toys, positioning and exercises and statementing. Advisers will give individual advice to families concerning continence, education, mobility, benefits and medical issues.

The Bobath Centre for Children with Cerebral Palsy

250 East End Road
London N2 8AU
Tel: 0181 444 3355
Fax: 0181 444 3399

Specifically for children with cerebral palsy. Aims to encourage and increase the child's ability to move and function as normally as possible using the Bobath technique which the centre has developed.

Brainwave Centre

Huntworth Gate
Bridgewater
Somerset TA6 6LQ
Tel: 01278 429089
Fax: 01278 429622
Website: www.brainwave.org.uk

For brain-injured children and adults. Designs individual tailored programmes of rehabilitation therapy which are carried out at home with help from family and volunteers for up to 15 hours per week.

Breakthrough Trust – Deaf Hearing Integration

Alan Geale House
The Close
Westhill Campus
Bristol Road
Selly Oak
Birmingham B29 6LN
Tel (minicom and voice): 0121 472 6447
Fax: 0121 415 2323

For deaf and hearing people who want to come together in the spirit of integration and understanding through training, social activities and contact groups. Offers courses using new technology for communication, family contact groups and after-school clubs.

British Deaf Association

1–3 Worship Street
London EC2A 2AB
Tel (voice): 0171 588 3520
Tel (minicom): 0171 588 3529
Fax: 0171 588 3527
Website: www.bda.org.uk

Promotes deaf people as equal partners in society and campaigns for the deaf community to be accepted as an integral part of British life with British Sign Language seen as an accepted minority language. Offers services in the following areas: education and youth, information and media access, advocacy, development in the community and health promotion. Members receive a regular newsletter with information on services and campaigns.

British Epilepsy Association

Anstey House
40 Hanover Square
Leeds
West Yorkshire LS3 1BE
Epilepsy Helpline: 0800 309030
Tel: 0113 243 9393
Fax: 0113 242 8804
E-mail: epilepsy@bea.org.uk
Website: www.epilepsy.org.uk

For people with epilepsy, their families and employers. Provides information on living with epilepsy, publications and an epilepsy helpline. Supports a network of 150 branches nationwide. Members receive a quarterly newsletter, free insurance scheme and access to helpline. Produces a range of leaflets including *Epilepsy and Children* and *Epilepsy and Swimming*, and videos on treatment and first aid.

British Heart Foundation

14 Fitzhardinge Street
London W1H 4DH
Tel: 0171 935 0185
Fax: 0171 486 5820

Provides information for adults and children with heart conditions. Also conducts research, promotes a healthy lifestyle and funds equipment, staff and rehabilitation programmes.

The British Institute for Brain Injured Children

Knowle Hall
Knowle
Bridgewater
Somerset TA7 8PJ
Tel: 01278 684060
Fax: 01278 685573

Teaches parents of brain-injured children stimulation therapy which they can practise at home after assessment.

British Institute of Learning Difficulties

Wolverhampton Road
Kidderminster
Worcs DY10 3PP
Tel: 01562 850251
Fax: 01562 851970
E-mail: bild@bild.demon.co.uk

For anyone working with people with a learning disability. Publishes books and the *British Journal of Learning Disabilities* and provides training.

British Society for Music Therapy

25 Rosslyn Ave
East Barnet
Herts EN4 8DH
Tel/fax: 0181 368 8879
E-mail: Denize@BSMT.demon.co.uk

For all those with an interest in music therapy. Holds meetings, workshops and conferences, produces journals and bulletins and has a comprehensive catalogue of books on all aspects of music therapy.

Brittle Bone Society

30 Guthrie Street
Dundee DD1 5BS
Tel: 01382 204446/7
Fax: 01382 206771

Promotes research into brittle bone diseases and provides support and advice to sufferers and their families. Organizes local meetings and an annual conference for the exchange of ideas. Produces a regular newsletter and gives advice on grants, education, equipment and genetics. Raises money to help fund necessary equipment and can sometimes help with other financial needs such as for hospital visiting and holidays.

Carers National Association

20–25 Glasshouse Yard
London EC1A 4JS
Tel: 0171 490 8818
Fax: 0171 490 8824

Provides information, advice and support to carers. Campaigns for greater awareness in government and society for the needs of carers and for action to be taken to support them. Provides an information pack for members and a magazine on new developments. Has a network of branches and groups to support carers and provides an opportunity to share experience and information. Produces a range of booklets and publications on benefits, combining caring and work and making life easier.

Centre for Studies in Inclusive Education

1 Redland Close
Elm Lane
Redland
Bristol BS6 6UE
Tel: 0117 923 8450
Fax: 0117 923 8460
E-mail: 100432.3417@compuserve.com

Aims to increase the number of children with special needs who are educated in mainstream schools. Produces a range of publications on the theory and practice of integrating children.

Children's Head Injury Trust

c/o Neurosurgery
The Radcliffe Infirmary
Woodstock Road
Oxford OX2 6HE
Tel/fax: 01865 224786
E-mail: enquiries@chit.demon.co.uk

For children with acquired brain injury (i.e. not birth defects), their families and professionals. Provides advice, information on brain injury and special schools. Supports research and has a hardship fund.

Children's Legal Centre

University of Essex
Wivenhoe Park
Colchester
Essex CO4 3SQ
Tel: 01206 873820 (advice: Mon–Fri, 2–5pm)
Tel: 01206 872466 (admin)
Fax: 01206 874026
E-mail: clc@essex.ac.uk

Runs a free and confidential legal advice and information service covering all aspects of the law and policy affecting children and young people. The Education Legal Advocacy Unit provides advice and representation to parents in education disputes with a school or local education authority. Operates within south-east England but can still provide advice and negotiation and mediation services outside this area. Produces a range of information sheets and guides.

The Children's Trust

Tadworth Court
Tadworth
Surrey KT20 5RU
Tel: 01737 357171
Fax: 01737 371244

For babies and children with profound disabilities and complex medical needs. Provides residential care service for short- or medium-term periods, a care and therapy service, a hospice service and outreach care. Services are run by an interdisciplinary team including medical staff, therapists and teachers in conjunction with parents.

Cystic Fibrosis Trust

11 London Road
Bromley
Kent BR1 1BY
Tel: 0181 464 7211
Fax: 0181 313 0472

For people with cystic fibrosis (CF), their families and professionals. Provides support for CF sufferers and their families including information, a magazine and notices of local meetings. Also funds research and clinics and raises awareness. Has a mail-order list of publications on CF and physiotherapy, diet, financial help, school, genetics etc.

Deafblind UK

> 100 Bridge Street
> Peterborough PE1 1DY
> Tel and Minicom: 01733-358100
> Fax: 01733 358356
> Qwerty: 01733 358858
> Helpline: 0800 132320
> E-mail: jackie@deafblnd.demon.co.uk

For those who experience difficulties with sight and hearing. Offers training for deafblind people and in deafblind awareness, also advice, counselling and information. Produces newsletters and arranges holidays.

DELTA Deaf Education through Listening and Talking

> PO Box 20
> Haverhill
> Suffolk CB9 7BD
> Tel: 01440 783689

Promotes the natural aural approach, i.e. children are given hearing aids or cochlear implants to enhance what hearing they have and encouraged to develop spoken language by copying what they hear rather than use sign language. Helps families with severely or profoundly deaf children who want those children to acquire natural, effective spoken language. The aim is that deaf children will then have access to the hearing world rather than being 'confined' to the deaf world. Provides workshops, meetings and summer schools, also a range of factsheets and booklets.

Disabled Living Foundation

> 380–384 Harrow Road
> London W9 2HU
> Tel: 0171 289 6111
> Fax: 0171 266 2922
> Helpline: 0870 603 9177
> Minicom: 0870 603 9176
> E-mail: dlfinfo@dlf.org.uk
> Website: www.dlf.org.uk

Provides information on equipment for disabled people. Offers a telephone helpline and responds to written enquiries. Has an equipment centre displaying equipment for people to try out. Also produces a range of publications on choosing and using equipment and on suppliers, e.g. 'children's play equipment', 'mobility equipment' and 'everyday living equipment'.

Down's Syndrome Association

155 Mitcham Road
London SW17 9PG
Tel: 0181 682 4001
Fax: 0181 682 4012
E-mail: downs-syndrome.org.uk

For people with Down's Syndrome, their parents and interested professionals. Provides information and support, a quarterly newsletter and leaflets and has a network of branches and groups which can provide contact with other parents. An under-fives conference is held annually. Has a comprehensive mail-order book list as well as leaflets on, for instance, finding out that your baby has Down's.

Down's Ed: The Down's Syndrome Educational Trust

The Sarah Duffen Centre
Belmont Street
Southsea
Portsmouth
Hants PO5 1NA
Tel: 01705 824261
Fax: 01705 824265
E-mail: enquiries@downsnet.org
Website: www.downsnet.org/

Aims to promote development of children and young people with Down's. Funds original research, provides direct services to families and disseminates information through publishing and training activities. Provides publications on subscription, training events (e.g. early development, behaviour management), psychological assessments, consultancy, a catalogue of books and educational materials.

The Dyscovery Centre for Dyspraxia, Dyslexia and Associated Learning Difficulties

12 Cathedral Road
Cardiff CF1 9LJ
Tel: 01222 788666
Fax: 01222 788604

Aims to provide a multi-disciplinary assessment and treatment service to meet the needs of each child with dyspraxia, dyslexia or associated learning difficulties. Provides assessment and treatment on site as well as home programmes. Provides training courses for professionals and publications e.g. *Dyspraxia – Diagnosis in the Pre-school Child, Dyspraxia – Play Activities for the Pre-school Child.*

Dyspraxia Foundation

8 West Alley
Hitchin
Herts SG5 1EG
Tel: 01462 455016
Fax: 01462 455052
Website: www.emmbrook.demon.co.uk/dysprax/ homepage.htm

Aims to support individuals with dyspraxia and their families. Acts as an information and resource centre, offering support and advice to parents. Promotes rapid diagnosis and treatment and a wider understanding, especially among health and education professionals. Produces a range of articles, leaflets and booklets including *Living with Dyspraxia – Handy Tips, Children with Developmental Dyspraxia: Information for Parents / Teachers.*

Elizabeth Foundation

> Southwick Hill Road
> Cosham
> Portsmouth PO6 3LL
> Hants
> Tel: 01705 372735
> Fax: 01705 326155

Provides a family centre for hearing impaired pre-school children and their families. This teaches children to develop their communication skills and teaches parents to help their children with speech and language. Provides help and support for parents and runs a correspondence course for parents to learn about communication, child development and games and activities for thinking, listening and speech. Also runs nursery classes for children aged up to five. Has a music studio which provides musical auditory training and trains parents and teachers. Another Elizabeth Foundation is to be built in Bradford, West Yorkshire.

Friends for Young Deaf People

> FYD Communication Centre
> East Court Mansion
> Council Offices
> College Lane
> East Grinstead RH19 3LT
> Tel (voice): 01342 323444
> Tel (minicom): 01342 312639
> Fax: 01342 410232

Aims to bring together deaf and hearing young people for personal development and communication. Also works with children and families. Organizes family weekends, training programmes and deaf awareness workshops.

Henshaw's Society for the Blind

> John Derby House
> 88–92 Talbot Road
> Old Trafford
> Manchester M16 0GS
> Tel: 0161 872 1234
> Fax: 0161 848 9889
> E-mail: henry@henshaws.demon.co.uk

For people with a visual impairment and their families. Based in the north of England. Has a family support officer who visits families offering support. Provides information and advice, organizes social activities for the whole family. Strong emphasis on the whole family, not just the child with a visual impairment.

High/Scope

Copperfield House
190–192 Maple Road
London SE20 8HT
Tel: 0181 676 0220

Responsible for the High/Scope system used in schools and playgroups and Caring Start ideas used in the home. Provides information and training. See pages 84–86.

I CAN

Barbican City Gate
1–3 Dufferin Street
London EC1Y 8NA
Tel: 0171 374 4422
Fax: 0171 374 2762

Works principally with children with a speech or language disorder by running schools and nurseries. Organizes a range of courses for teachers, teaching assistants and speech therapists and produces books and pamphlets on language teaching. In addition I CAN runs the only school in the UK for children with severe eczema or asthma.

Information Exchange

39 Britannia Road
Kingswood BS15 2BG
Tel/fax: 0117 961 9144
E-mail: brills@compuserve.com

For families and professionals living or working with children and young adults who have sensory impairments and other complex needs. Produces a magazine three times per year which offers support, advice and information to readers and offers them the opportunity to write articles and letters and submit ideas.

IPSEA Independent Panel for Special Education Advice

22 Warren Hill Road
Woodbridge
Suffolk IP12 4DU
Tel: 01394 380518 (admin and fax)
Tel: 01394 382814 (advice)

Provides independent advice on local education authorities' (LEA) duties to provide for children with special educational needs. Also provides second professional opinions for parents who disagree with the LEA's assessment of their child. Offers advice and representation at Special Needs Tribunals for those appealing against an LEA decision.

ISEA Independent Special Education Advice (Scotland)

164 High Street
Dalkeith
Mid Lothian EH22 1AY
Tel: 0131 665 7080 (advice)

As IPSEA above but for Scotland.

LASER The Language of Sign as an Educational Resource

Blenheim Centre
Crowther Place
Leeds LS6 2ST

For parents, educators and researchers who wish to develop the use of sign language in education. Promotes bilingual education – the use of BSL and English. Holds workshops throughout the country and national conferences on bilingual education. Members receive a newsletter and conference reports.

Limbless Association

Roehampton Rehabilitation Centre
Roehampton Lane
London SW15 5PR
Tel: 0181 788 1777
Fax: 0181 788 3444
E-mail: limbassc@aol.com
Website: www.charitynet.org/~limbassoc

Provides information and advice for those who have been born without upper or lower limbs or who have had amputations. Nationwide network offering support and encouragement. Sponsors research and development in rehabilitation services and limb technology. Produces a quarterly magazine.

LOOK, National Federation of Families with Visually Impaired Children

Queen Alexandra College
49 Court Oak Road
Harborne
Birmingham B17 9TG
Tel: 0121 428 5038

Provides support and information for families of visually impaired children through local groups. Publishes a quarterly newsletter plus access to information on issues such as education, benefits and equipment.

Makaton Vocabulary Development Project

31 Firwood Drive
Camberley
Surrey GU15 3QD
Tel: 01276 61390
Fax: 01276 681368
E-mail: mvdp@makaton.org
Website: www.makaton.org

Makaton is a communication system using the spoken word and signs. Created for children and adults with communication difficulties, it aims to give a visual prompt alongside speech and symbols. Acts as the administrative centre for the Makaton signing system. Has a mail-order catalogue of publications including books of the signs and symbols, a Parent Carer Makaton Distance Training Pack plus the signed Nursery Rhyme video with Dave Benson Phillips. Organizes courses on Makaton given by accredited teachers.

Mencap

123 Golden Lane
London EC1Y 0RT
Tel: 0171 454 0454
Tel: 0171 696 5593 (Infoline)
Fax: 0171 608 3254

For all people with a learning disability and their families. Provides support and help for parents through its divisional offices and local societies. Family Adviser Service offers help and advice when a family finds out a child has a learning disability or when it is faced with decisions about the future. Organizes Gateway Clubs to offer leisure opportunities to children and adults with learning difficulties. Has a campaigning role to improve public awareness and services for people with learning disabilities. Has a comprehensive mail-order book catalogue.

Muscular Dystrophy Group

7–11 Prescott Place
London SW4 6BS
Tel: 0171 720 8055
Fax: 0171 498 0670

Provides information and support through local branches and support groups. A telephone information service and a nationwide team of family care officers give specialist advice. Provides occupational therapy advice on equipment and a fund is available for essential equipment. Publishes booklets on physiotherapy, equipment and housing adaptations as well as a newsletter. Funds eight muscle centres around the country.

Music and the Deaf

Kirklees Media Centre
7 Northumberland Street
Huddersfield HD1 1RL
Tel: 01484 425551
Fax: 01484 425560

Helps hearing-impaired people gain access to music and related performing arts either as active performers or as listeners and observers. Produces a list of performances nationwide which will be signed and a publications list *All Join In: Musical Activities for Hearing Impaired Children* and *Music for Deaf Children: A Practical Guide for Parents, Teachers and Others.*

National Association of Toy and Leisure Libraries: Play Matters

68 Churchway
London NW1 1LT
Tel: 0171 387 9592
Fax: 0171 383 2714
Website: www.charitynet.org/~NATLL

Parent body for over 1000 toy libraries in UK. These libraries provide good-quality carefully chosen toys for young children and often include more specialist toys for those with special needs. They offer a supportive befriending service to parents. Contact above address with SAE for the address of your nearest toy library. Has a mail-order catalogue of books and leaflets on play and special needs.

National Asthma Campaign

Providence House
Providence Place
London N1 0NT
Tel: 0171 226 2260
Fax: 0171 704 0740
Asthma Helpline: 01345 010203
Website: www.asthma.org.uk

Provides information and support to people with asthma, their families and professionals. Also promotes and funds research and campaigns to raise awareness of the condition. Has a helpline staffed by specialist nurses, a network of local branches and a magazine. There is a Junior Asthma Club for children aged 4–12. Produces a range of publications.

National Autistic Society

393 City Road
London EC1V 1NE
Tel: 0171 833 2299
Fax: 0171 833 9666
E-mail: nas@clusl.ulcc.ac.uk
Website: www.oneworld.org/autism_uk

Provides information and support for those with autism and their families. Has a publications list and newsletter. Local branches also offer information and support. Aims to provide educational and support services for autistic people hence it runs schools, adult units, a diagnostic and assessment centre as well as a supported employment scheme. It also runs training courses and conferences geared more towards professionals.

National Blind Children's Society

Nat West Chambers
Victoria Street
Burnham on Sea
Somerset TA8 1AN
Tel: 01278 793792
Fax: 01278 792929
E-mail: nbcs@th.newnet.co.uk
Website: www.nbcs.org.uk

For children with visual impairment from 0 to 18. Can provide equipment and support for parents and advice on education. Will help raise funds for the purchase of equipment for visually impaired children.

National Children's Bureau

8 Wakeley Street
London EC1V 7QE
Tel: 0171 843 6000
Fax: 0171 278 9512

Aims to identify and promote the interests of all children and improve their status through research, policy development and the promotion of good practice in education, social work and health care. Has an extensive library and information service, a programme of conferences and seminars and publishes books.

National Deaf Children's Society

15 Dufferin Street
London EC1Y 8PD
Tel: 0171 250 0123 (information and helpline)

For families of children with any hearing loss. Provides information and advice and practical support through a network of regional staff and trained local representatives. Produces a Family Information Pack for families with a child who has been recently diagnosed deaf. Produces a range of pamphlets.

National Institute of Conductive Education

Cannon Hill House
Russell Road
Moseley
Birmingham B13 8RD
Tel: 0121 449 1569
Fax: 0121 449 1611
E-mail: foundation@conductive-education.org.uk

Offers a parent and child service and a nursery group for pre-school children with cerebral palsy and other neurological disorders. Uses the principles of conductive education.

National Portage Association

Administrator – Mrs Brenda Paul
127 Monks Dale
Yeovil
Somerset BA21 3JE
Tel: 01935 471641 (Mon and Thur, 9–1pm)

For parents and professionals who use portage. Oversees portage nationally, setting a code of practice for portage services. Provides and monitors training programmes in portage, holds a conference and produces a newsletter.

National Society for Epilepsy

Chalfont St Peter
Gerrards Cross
Bucks SL9 0RJ
Tel: 01494 601300
Helpline: 01494 601400
Fax: 01494 871927
Website: www.erg.ion.ucl.ac.uk/nsehome

For anybody with an interest in epilepsy. Has an information and education service which provides a range of leaflets on epilepsy, its treatment, complementary therapies, welfare benefits etc. Also works to raise public awareness, offers a network of support groups and runs a range of residential and medical services.

NCH Action for Children

85 Highbury Park
London N5 1UD
Tel: 0171 226 2033
Fax: 0171 226 2537
Website: www.nchafc.org.uk

Aims to improve the quality of life for the most vulnerable children and young people in society including children with special needs. Run a range of projects, usually with health, education or social services, including supporting children with special needs in the community, family centres, respite care and residential schools.

Network 81

1–7 Woodfield Terrace
Stansted
Essex CM24 8AJ
Tel: 01279 647415 (Mon–Fri, 10am–2pm)
Fax: 01279 816438

A national network of parents of children with special needs established to advance the education of children with special needs and to keep parents informed of education matters. It aims for inclusive education but will support parental choice. It keeps abreast of new policies and law. It has a helpline, Befrienders, and publishes a *Step by Step Guide to Statementing*.

PEACH Parents for the Early Intervention of Autism in Children

PO Box 10836
London SW13 9JB
Fax: 0181 286 7049
E-mail: peach@clara.net
Website: www.peach.uk.com

Provides support and information for parents practising the home-based early intervention therapy devised by Dr Lovaas in the US. Follows a behavioural approach rewarding good behaviour rather than punishing bad, requires 35–40 hours of one-on-one intensive instruction each week from a team of tutors in your own home.

PLANET (Play Leisure Advice Network)

Cambridge House
Cambridge Grove
London W6 0LE
Tel: 0181 741 4054
Fax: 0181 741 4505
Website: www.oneworld.org/scf/planet

An information resource on play, leisure and recreation for children, young people and adults with disabilities. Provides information and advice on play, leisure equipment, books, videos and suppliers. Also provides training and displays at conferences. Provides an information pack and publications list and you can also write and ask for a database search for your child's particular needs.

Pre-school Learning Alliance

69 King's Cross Road
London WC1X 9LL
Tel: 0171 833 0991
Fax: 0171 837 4942
E-mail: pla@pre-school.org.uk

Supports the establishment and running of community run pre-schools including Opportunity Groups. Provides information, publications and training on special needs for helpers in pre-schools and gives grants to fund one-to-one helpers for children with special needs.

Reach (Association for Children with Hand or Arm Deficiency)

12 Wilson Way
Earls Barton
Northants NN6 0NZ
Tel/fax: 01604 811041
E-mail: reach@reach.org.uk
Website: www.reach.org.uk

For families of children with upper limb problems and professionals. Provides information and publications including a quarterly newsletter, advice and support and access to other families in similar situations.

Research Trust for Metabolic Diseases in Children

Golden Gates Lodge
Weston Road
Crewe
Cheshire CW2 5XN
Tel: 01270 250221
Fax: 01270 250244

For families and professionals. Provides disease specific information, welfare advice, counselling, networking and publications. Also offers a regular newsletter and an annual conference.

Rett Syndrome Association UK

113 Friern Barnet Road
London N22 3EU
Tel: 0181 361 5161
Fax: 0181 368 6123
E-mail: rett assoc@aol.com

For families of children/women with Rett Syndrome. Runs an information service and publishes a newsletter. Has support groups, regional and national meetings including an annual conference. Holds diagnostic and management clinics.

Riding for the Disabled Association

Lavinia Norfolk House
Avenue R
National Agricultural Centre
Stoneleigh Park
Kenilworth
Warwicks CV8 2LY
Tel: 01203 696510
Fax: 01203 696532

Oversees the Riding for the Disabled Groups around the country. Puts parents in touch with local branches.

Royal Association for Disability and Rehabilitation (RADAR)

12 City Forum
250 City Road
London EC1V 8AF
Tel: 0171 250 3222
Fax: 0171 250 0212
Tel (minicom): 0171 250 4119
E-mail: radar@radar.org.uk
Website: www.radar.org.uk

For people with physical disabilities and those interested in disability issues. It provides information and advice and campaigns for the rights and needs of disabled people. It is particularly involved with education, health, social services, employment, holidays, housing and mobility. Has a publications list which includes *Holidays, Mobility* and *Children First: A Guide to the Needs of Disabled Children in School*. Members receive a monthly bulletin.

Royal National Institute for the Blind

224 Great Portland Street
London W1N 6AA
Tel: 0171 388 1266
Fax: 0171 383 4821
E-mail: rnib.org.uk

For visually impaired people, their families and those who work with them. Offers a number of services. Education Information Service provides information and advice and will put parents in touch with other RNIB professionals or statutory services. Has a wide range of publications and fact sheets on education and welfare and publishes its own magazines. RNIB runs Education Centres in five locations

which hold educational technology, toys, games etc. They provide training for parents, specialist assessments and technology services. There is also an advocacy service. Runs five schools for children aged 2–19 but will also support visually impaired children in mainstream education. Also provides information on toys and play ideas (such as the book *Look and Touch*), on different eye conditions and their treatment and specialist products.

SCOPE

PO Box 833
Milton Keynes MK14 6DR
Tel: 0800 626216
Fax: 01908 691702
E-mail: cphelpline@scope.org.uk
Website: www.scope.org.uk

Offers services for people with cerebral palsy and their families including information and advice through a Helpline and parent information leaflets, a library and an assessment service. It has local groups and a network of fieldworkers. It has a Schools for Parents scheme to teach parents how to help their child based on conductive education principles.

Sense (The National Deafblind and Rubella Association)

11–13 Clifton Terrace
London N4 3SR
Tel: 0171 272 7774
Fax: 0171 272 6012
email: enquiries@sense.org.uk

Supports and campaigns for the deafblind and their families. Runs a network of family centres, regional advisory services and branches. Trains Intervenors to work one-on-one to help children and adults develop and explore the world. Offers specialist assessment, nursery and school support, training for parents and help with statementing. Publishes its own magazines and has a booklist which includes *Deafblind Infants and Children: A Developmental Guide*.

The Signalong Group

Communication and Language Centre
North Pond Side Historic Dockyard
Chatham
Kent ME4 4TY
Tel: 01634 819915

Signalong is a sign-supporting system based on British Sign Language and designed to help children and adults with learning disabilities to acquire language skills and to aid where there are communication difficulties. Runs courses throughout the country (contact the above address) which introduce techniques for teaching communication skills to people with learning difficulties and the Signalong methodology. See p.00 for using signs.

Sound Learning Centre

12 The Rise
London N13 5LE
Tel/fax: 0181 882 1060

Offers Auditory Integration Training, Lightwave Stimulation, and Neuro-Developmental Delay Remediation for children and adults with learning and sensory difficulties. Offers informal briefings to introduce the treatments, demonstrate equipment, present case studies and professional evaluations.

Speech, Language and Hearing Centre

1–5 Christopher Place
Chalton Street
London NW1 1JF
Tel: 0171 383 3834
Fax: 0171 383 3099

For children under five with a hearing impairment or delay in communication. Offers assessment and therapy, support and guidance for parents and a nursery curriculum and therapy or clinical therapy sessions from an interdisciplinary team.

Alfred A Tomatis Foundation

3 Wallands Crescent
Lewes
East Sussex BN7 2QT
Tel: 01273 474877
Fax: 01273 487500
E-mail: tomatis-foundation@btinternet.com

Based on the idea that some children with disorders such as autism or epilepsy have their listening senses distorted which in turn distorts neurological patterns and exacerbates developmental disorders. The Tomatis Method or 'auditory training' aims to re-educate the way we listen to improve learning and language abilities, communication, creativity and social behaviour.

VisionAid

22A Chorley New Road
Bolton BL1 4AP
Tel: 01204 531882
Fax: 01204 394218

Established by a group of parents to provide advice, information and support for visually impaired children, their families and professionals. Services include an information and reference library, specialist toy loan and visual stimulation equipment, hi-tech aid and tactile photocopying. A helpline is available for information and support and guidance can be given on such issues as education and benefits.

Visual Impairment Support and Advisory Service

14 Pimlott Grove
Prestwich
Manchester M25 9TR
Tel: 0161 773 0869

A contact support and resource service for families of blind and visually impaired babies and children. Puts parents in contact with others who have a similarly affected child. Believes that children benefit from education from birth and therefore helps parents to get their child referred to all relevant professionals as early as possible. Provides telephone counselling, advice on issues such as education and welfare rights. Area co-ordinators in various parts of the country befriend families and visit, offering support and practical advice on toys and equipment.

Young Arthritis Care

18 Stephenson Way
London NW1 2HD
Tel: 0171 916 1500
Fax: 0171 916 1505

Part of Arthritis Care for the under 45s. Provides information, advice and publications on such subjects as diet, exercise and pain management. Has a nationwide network of contacts, including parent contacts who can give help and support. Local groups also meet up and share information. Also runs confidence building courses for older children.

SUPPLIERS OF TOYS AND EQUIPMENT FOR CHILDREN WITH SPECIAL NEEDS

Child's Play (International)

Ashworth Road
Bridgemead
Swindon SN5 7YD
Tel: 01793 616286
Fax: 01793 512795

Educational books, games and audio-visual material

Galt Educational

Culvert Street
Oldham
Lancashire OL4 2GE
Tel: 0161 627 5086
Fax: 0161 627 1543
E-mail: enquiries@galt-education.co.uk

Wide range of toys, games and furniture

Hope Education

Orb Mill
Huddersfield Road
Waterhead
Oldham
Lancashire OL4 2ST
Tel: 0161 633 6611
Fax: 0161 633 3431
E-mail: enquiries@hope-education.co.uk

Toys and equipment for children including those with special needs. Includes fibre optics.

Mike Ayres Design

Unit 8
Shepherds Grove
Stanton
Bury St Edmunds
Suffolk IP31 2AR
Tel: 01359 251551
Fax: 01359 251707

Supplies soft play and sensory equipment

NES Arnold

Ludlow Hill Road
West Bridgford
Nottingham NG2 6HD
Tel: 0115 945 2201
Fax: 0500 410420

Supplies a wide range of toys and equipment to playgroups and pre-schools.

Nottingham Rehab

Ludlow Hill Road
West Bridgford
Nottingham NG2 6HD
Tel: 0115 945 2345
Fax: 0115 945 2124

Provides a mail order catalogue 'Ways and Means' of household products for people with special needs. Includes cutlery and crockery, special scissors and pencil grips. Also has a paediatric catalogue with equipment, games and toys for children with special needs.

Quest Enabling Designs

Ability House
242 Gosport Road
Fareham
Hants PO16 0SS
Tel: 01329 828444
Fax: 01329 828800

Supplies switches and wheelchairs

RNIB

PO Box 173
Peterborough
Tel: 0345 023153

Provides a toy catalogue and catalogue of products which include games, puzzles and leisure activities for children with a visual impairment.

ROMPA

Goyt Side Road
Chesterfield
Derbyshire S40 2PH
Tel: 0800 056 2323
Fax: 01246 221802
E-mail: sales@rompa.co.uk
Website: www.rompa.co.uk

Supplies mail-order toys, soft play and multi-sensory equipment for children with special needs.

Spacekraft Ltd

Cowgill House
Rosse Street
Shipley
West Yorks BD18 3SW
Tel: 01274 581007
Fax: 01274 531966
E-mail: gf36@dial.pipex.com

Supplies play equipment including sensory equipment for children with special needs.

TFH

76 Barracks Road
Sandy Lane Industrial Estate
Stourport on Severn
Worcs DY13 9QB
Tel: 01299 827820
Fax: 01299 827035
E-mail: tfhhq@globalnet.co.uk
Website: www.tfhuk.com

Provides a mail-order catalogue of fun, toys and games for children and adults with special needs.

Glossary

child development centre	centre for assessment and therapy attended by a variety of specialists.
eye pointing	the child looks specifically at something to show he wants it or in answer to a question, i.e. points using his gaze rather than his finger.
fine motor skills	movements of the hands and fingers.
gross motor skills	movements of the body and limbs.
hand-over-hand	placing your hands over your child's hands to get him to perform a required action such as bringing a spoon to his mouth.
Makaton	signing system and symbols used with children and adults with special needs.
object permanence	awareness that something continues to exist even when it can no longer be seen.
occupational therapist	helps with fine motor skills, feeding and dressing etc.
opportunity group	play group for children with special needs.
paediatrician	doctor with a specialism in child development and child health.
physiotherapist	helps with physical skills.
portage	home-based therapy programme.
respite care	when a carer looks after a child with special needs for a short period to give the family a break and introduce the child to new people.
Signalong	signing system and symbols used with children and adults with special needs.
speech and language therapist	helps with language, communication and sometimes eating.
TEACCH	Treatment and Education of Autistic and related Communication-handicapped CHildren – a system of structured teaching for children with autism and similar special needs.